ISBN 0-9623687-1-7

This publication is set in 12 point ITC Galliard Roman and Caflisch Script.

Printed in China

Cover Fountain Sculptor:
Manuel Palos Scultpture, Inc.
San Francisco, California

Publication design and prepatory by
Roy Minor

An afternoon in the patio garden of Sheila Bony visiting with Heidi Chadwick.

Artscapes

Harmony for Plants and People

By

James M. Chadwick

Squash Blossom

Dedication

It is with gratitude and humility that I dedicate this work to the memory of Paul Giuliana, who was born in Pietrapicia, Sicily, in 1912, and died in Barnstable, Massachusetts, in 1966. Dr. Giuliana was a man of exceptional strength, character and foresight. Having lost his vision early in life, he nevertheless prospered and achieved his personal goal of helping others through the arts. I first met him in the late 1950s, when he was a vital presence within the Boston and Cape Cod area music community. A few years later, he founded the Cape Cod Conservatory of Music.

When asked to design a garden for this extraordinary man, I did not attempt to become his eyes, but tried to tune into his other senses. Through him I learned to concentrate on what was available, rather than what was missing. Because of this experience I grew to understand that, in this world, I do not need to "keep my eyes open" but rather to close them and open my mind.

James M. Chadwick

An "Art Deco" ranch-style residence is entered through this magnificent gate, 48" in width and nearly 7' high with a screen back.

Table of Contents

Preface

I t is an old remark that "all arts and sciences have a mutual dependence upon each other". Thus, men, very different in genius and pursuits, become mutually subservient to each other, and a very useful kind of commerce is established by which the old arts are improved, and new ones invented.

William Brownrigg *The Art of Making Common Salt*, London, 1748

Inventing new art while pursuing the old one follows no rules. Each time a finger is lifted to sketch a thought, it is possible that the idea may change at a moment's notice. Artist's painting will find their idea changed from the instant it leaves the brain to its final impulse from the brush to one's canvass taking a journey of micro-seconds. It is good to know that one is free to move artistically. This freedom of expression allows a design to be left as is or slightly cultivated for simplicity and ingenuity.

The ensuing text and photographs show small and larger residential areas, each design incorporating as much simplicity as possible, while expressing the needs of the client. Use of color and textured patterns are the key in successful garden designs.

The residential environment of houses, estates, apartments, or farms should be reflective of the individuals. The design should always be spiritual, which is done by going beyond the usual artistic and emotional scope of the assignment, or as quietly known in design vocabulary as restraint and good taste.

Good art takes a journey of life. The more activity one has, the more inventive and restrained the art behaves. It's a life's collection of travel, education, social enterprise and reading. Combine these separate journeys into art and spiritual boundaries and the results will be an honest introspection for very successful designs.

Swimming hole or reflecting pool? A stone masonry retaining wall stabilizes the cut and serves as a reflecting image when the water is not in use. The reflective value is enhanced by a green/black plaster coating on the pool walls. The small redwood decking creates a natural transition to the woodsy background.

"This was one of my first experiences with California pools and people. The design put the pool on a lower elevation, which was prescribed by the client and the pool people before I arrived on the scene, but it actually was the only space available. The pool was built along with its retaining wall, then we came up with the design ideas. Along the way I found out that the area reminded the owner of an old swimming hole where he played as a child, thus the idea enhanced the design by incorporating the long oak limb hanging over the 'pond' and providing a diving rock. The deck arrangements were of wood under the trees and exposed aggregate in the sunny places. A wood patio was built on top of the retaining wall, which was in closer proximity to the house, giving one a great feeling of viewing the 'pond' and enjoying the environs."

A view from the bedroom suite captures the full sweep of the garden. Space for family entertaining is abundant. A small White Birch copse provides both sight and sound values on quiet evenings. On the right, a garden path of annuals and espaliered fruit trees separate the lawn area from the herb and vegetable gardens.

An informal entrance is made of Arizona flagstone with joints of Irish Moss and dwarf Mugo Pine with Cotoneaster (horizontalis) strategically placed to modify traffic to the left.

A bird, flower and small animal garden sanctuary creates a quiet place to exercise all the physical and aural senses. A medium brown slate is surrounded by a ground cover of Veronica repens, a creeper with a small white flower that blooms for most of the season. Azaleas, White Dogwood, Tasmanian Fern, Sarcocococa and Choisya ternate are a few of the many plants with distinct seasonal virtues in the mini-sitting areas.

Statues within plantings are always effective. The background riprap wall, using fieldstone of head size, is laid on an angle against the grade cut. The color is a pleasant background support for the garden flowers and foliage. The Roman gladiator amidst the Hydrangea , sparks the imagination. The lower photo shows the stones separated just enough for chinking small favorites.

"REQUIREMENTS WERE TO REMOVE EXIST-
ING DOG HOUSE, barbeque and herb garden.
Considerations were then made for the lighting, drainage, separating the garden from
pool, spa and separate front entrance. We had
an all woman crew doing this work.

The client was a very charismatic, yet
private person, with a multifarious mind-set.
A look around her rooms showed the diversity
of interest about her personality.

The terrain was quite flat and
squeezed into a corner lot. With not much
room, the construction progress had to go
from back to front as there was only one
way to enter the property.

Four separate gardens were designed with
three levels of grade. The front entrance was
oriental with shoji screens separating the entrance on the other side. The other side was a
Moroccan garden with a floor fountain which
splashed softly enough to be heard around to
the other areas. This garden was available
only from the library. The next garden was
accessible from the 'Maroc' garden by walking
through a small Alice-in-Wonderland type
door. This area was adjacent to her kitchen.
A large 'Barby' was nearby and was attached
to a semicircular vine covered arbor. In the
center of this area was a sunken terrace with
a sitting wall which was actually an extension of the perimeter gardens of the Arbor,
barbeque and also of the Herb garden (also
vegetables). This garden has a fronted wood
piece for drying the herbs and/or vegetables.
The bottom part of the drying boards were
tiles depicting fruits and vegetables.

Leaving this garden one took some stone
steps up to a level area and suddenly looked
down to the pool and spa area. Entering
through a gate one felt the privacy and enjoyed the different fragrances of Lilac, etc."

*The fountain splashes quietly on the
stone table and runs down
the sides falling on the tile
re-circulation tub.*

4

A child's sand pit is surrounded by plantings for color and fragrance, in addition to a replica of a Rodin sculpture. A miniature rooftop in the background opens up for storing the child's toys.

The brick wall on the right extends down to a Japanese garden used for tea and quiet conversation.

"CALLED IN TO RE-DESIGN THEIR BACK YARD. The project existed on a sloping piece of ground going away from the rear to a distance of about two hundred feet. An unattached office and apartment cottage was near the house, as well as a greenhouse with an attached garage/tool house.

An interim passing-through garden, formal social terrace, perennial, and annual garden, child play area and a future pool, connected by walk, were the client's needs.

There wasn't much participation in this project by the husband. 'It's her project,' he would say. He was around quite a bit due to his at-home type of business computer connection with his office, and became vastly interested in the irrigation and drainage systems. Both quite pleasant but I felt a separation in their communication, yet tenderness toward each other. This type of situation is always difficult for an artist. Being absolute about your enthusiasm is never present and decisions are usually grey, never quite articulated.

It was her design and all the art with it. She was attractive, reluctant to decide, yet had good color sense about what she wanted and followed the book on most technical matters to do with the landscape. 'You give me the art and I'll do the rest kind of desire'."

This bird, flower and small animal garden sanctuary creates a quiet place to exercise all the senses. A medium brown slate is surrounded by a ground cover of Veronica repens, a creeper with a small white flower that blooms for most of the season. Azaleas, White Dogwood, Tasmanian Fern, Sarcococca and Choisya ternate are a few of the many plants with distinct seasonal virtues in the mini-sitting areas.

"*THIS JOB CAME BY WAY OF ONE OF THE SALESMEN at a pool company whose firm had done the concrete decking for the 60'
lap pool. The owner had already brought in hundreds of yards of gravel to fill up a huge valley in order to have a level area in
which to sit.*

*The house was a Frank Lloyd Wright design of concrete spaces and curves, quite austere inside, indeed, cold. The pool
coping and spa were already in place, surrounded by garaging areas on one side and a steep slope on the other. We provided
a design which employed the use of deep piers for deck supports and thus were able to find level space for family use. While
making this deck, we had a few large water washed boulders lifted over the garage and placed at various positions on the
deck which helped simulate a tranquil sea. The deck area consisted of long pieces of 1"x2" arranged in slow movement curves
like water currents. Occasionally we would insert some pieces of 1"x2" Redwood in place of Fir, in order to accentuate the
patterns and offer relief to the deck space. The deck railing was all Redwood which enabled the viewer to look through to
the natural landscape without being distracted by a lighter color of other wood.*"

"THIS PROJECT IS CONFINED SOLELY TO THE FRONT YARD which measured only 22'x25'. Its cost to the client was a little more than $17,000 (1987). It was probably the most difficult of designs to produce, considering house architecture, garage placement, house and garage balance (architectural), proximity to the street, narrowness of the lot, existing narrow brick walk and budget. Their budget was realistic, not fictitious in trying to keep it down, in that the amount allocated ($15,000) was in proportion to the value of its worth. I wasn't optimistic that anything much could be done under the budget restrictions. However, due to their sense of values and sensitivity to using unusual materials, it worked.

The leading factor here was the English Cottage style of the house which gave it a very low informal comfortable look. The next permanent item was the little narrow brick walk which was a bit rickety looking, yet showed some charm if only it could be uncovered. The slanting roofs, although shingled, would normally in England be thatched or made with slate. One would visualize slate or thatch (even if it wasn't) if the projection of everything else was present. These kinds of concepts come from some experience in theatre and painting theatre scenery where images are mindfully created to completion by basic outlines of a familiar study or scene.

The dry wall chinked with mosses, the interesting little fence on top of the wall which is lighter in weight than the wall, the nice effect of the hanging light and the curved wall entrance paved with hand-cut bricks in different sizes, all finalized and created a Monet like scene. Green hedging was used to accelerate the axis view to the front door which was at least 50' away. The hedging enhanced the walk and helped pull together all the other elements without dominating the scene."

This estate possesses many levels of garden to express the owner's various interests. Winding and serpentine walks reveal a surprise garden and statuary elements. The surfaces consist of a solid mix of fine sand and 1/4" gravel compacted. The color of the mix is important for retaining the interest of the wanderer. No dull drab colors here! These slow and easy paths allow one to meander through shadows, colors and smells - dreaming while in motion.

Two slate walls come together to frame a step. Filled with chinks of Artemisia, rock plants, a sense of completeness is achieved.

9

Planting the Seeds of an Art Form

In addition to the rewards inherent in seeing a plan on paper grow into a garden in bloom, I have enjoyed interpreting the broad level of introspection and involvement of people who want to improve their relationship with Nature. Much of my own personal experience of growth is interwoven into my business strategies: the business of supplementing meaning, empathizing with and evoking the experiences of others and expressing all of this in the form of landscape art.

At the beginning of a project, exactly what is to be done for a design is never quite understood, except in the very broadest sense of renewing an old garden, upgrading an existing design, providing a particular change in building use or starting from scratch. At the core of design development, the most essential thing is to learn more about the client and, for this, I have employed the use of field trips.

I first got the idea for these trips during my own student days in design study at Cornell University. During these informal full or half-day outings I took the client to a nursery, lumberyard, brick or stone source or maybe a leisurely walk through the woods. This experience gave and sustained a very personal interaction between the client and designer.

11

Bringing the beach to you! A Queen palm and ample white sand provide a place to lounge or picnic by the pool (See page 130 for pool and diving rock).

Amorphous ideas are shaped which act as a kind of therapy, with discussions that release a storehouse of reminiscences, personal insights and values. When the design is implemented, the final result will closely model the personality and characteristics of the client.

Gender differences can create conflict in meaning, manner of conversation and negotiating styles. In dealing with a couple, the designer must be adroit in aligning these differences for the best interpretation. The more attentive and sensitive the designer, the more balance can be achieved between experiences and idiosyncrasies. Rather than posing a drawback to creativity, this is how new ideas can be born and imagined.

A higher art is realized through discussion and experimentation. The closer you are to your subject, the more truthful the art. 🌼

This collage represents mini-sections of separate areas within landscaped front and rear sections. The white trellis is connected to a curved open-faced 3' dry wall. A small 18" stone passage leads to a private sunning area. Two facing Adirondack chairs within a small brick square await the Fourth of July parade.

*"I NOTED SHE HAD MANY MAGAZINE
ADS OF MINE STUCK IN HER NOTEBOOK.
The families had been in the area for
three generations.*

*The land consisted of about two
acres on a corner lot with the main
ranch house, out buildings and a major
studio which she used for her book bind-
ery business. The lot was divided into an
orchard on one side and their personal
pursuits on the other with a small lawn
in front.*

*The first effort was to establish their
character preference which was decid-
edly English. The front was opened up
to show a huge lawn area bordered by
perennials and annuals. The perimeter
of the entire lot was planted with an
evergreen hedge of 8' high Arborvitae.
Into this hedge was placed a 4' high
wire fence.*

*The rear gardens were framed by a
serpentine wall that began at 6' high
and ended at 3', due to the elevating
land grades. Actually, the top of the
wall was level from start to finish so
the wall took on a visual movement
that fascinated the eye, but more
to the point, it did not seem huge or
excessive due to this technique. The
addition to the house of a bedroom
wing added another perspective to
their indoor/outdoor style. Thus, an
adjacent brick patio was added raising
a brick wall from zero to 18" high separating this patio from the back lawn.*

Refer to **❶** on page 15.

Refer to **❷** on page 15.

*An interesting "closing" finial was added to the step wall which supported an embankment surrounding the new wing.
The brick patio, which was laid on fines, took on a very natural look by way of removing some of the bricks and planting
small or medium garden perennials in these areas.*

*There were many roses and old favorites such as Dogwoods, Rhododendrons, Azaleas (Exbury Hybrids), Honeysuckles,
Passion vines, Clemantis, Camellias, Golden Chain trees, and Magnolias added to the surrounding landscape.*

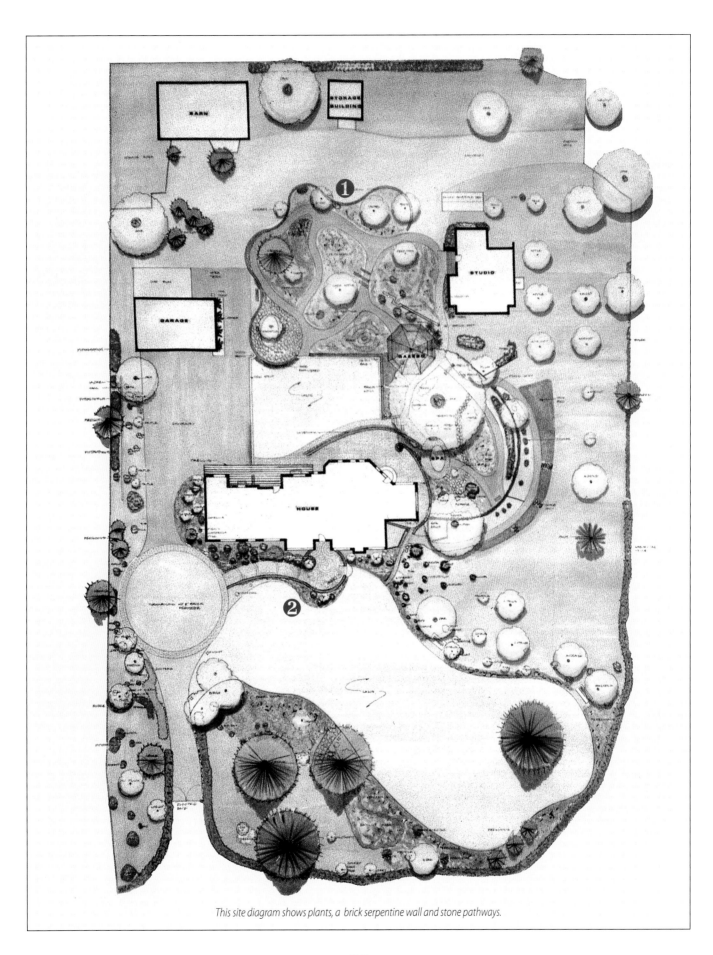

This site diagram shows plants, a brick serpentine wall and stone pathways.

From the main house, this loggia for living and entertaining is revealed at the end of an extended lawn.

The auto entrance to a fore court uses explicit visual language for identification from a busy road. The very strict geometric stone wall measures 4' x 4' x 5'. The 18" wrought iron fencing adds to the height as well as acting as an additional aesthetic element.

This lovely stone fountain was chiseled by a sculptor from South San Francisco, California. The stone was quarried in Southern Mexico and sculpted from the raw block. Varied earth colors fit into the ultimate Moorish plan for the walkways. The "water curtain" effect provides minimal sound and is a source of sparkling light either during the day or by moonlight. There are three of these beautiful fountains, one of which you will see on the cover of this publication.

17

When turning smaller spaces to maximum use, the most important rule is to use nonconflicting tones. In this patio off a bedroom, the steps down, which take up half the distance to the property line or fence, are white and do not interfere with the openness of the area. The slate floor is a softly mottled brown with pinkish tones to establish a solid pattern. The sitting wall has been constructed with white cement, mixed with white dolomite. A lattice, also painted white, has been erected against the screen fencing with espaliered vines and a redleaf Japanese Maple to conserve space.

A small water effect in one of the return fence corners offers a quiet and soothing recurring rhythm.

The outside of a fenced-in patio is planted with a three-tiered espaliered Rosa banksiana, a wonderful yellow climber. The vine itself keeps the desired form all year, although it only blooms for a month. To modify the accent after the blooming period, a clematis (Nellie Mosher) keeps the flowering pattern extending through the seasons.

This 10' by 10' gazebo is extended from an elevated surface decking and connected by a long catwalk with a railing on only one side. This keeps the structure distanced from the main deck but not visually constricted. The architectural style of the "broken hip" or "skirt" roof adds additional interest and minimizes bulk. The interior of the roof structure is made up of 2" x 6" rafters with a center pole which passes up through the roof to display a weather vane. Slats, nailed to the rafters are used to hold the cedar shingles. These 1" x 4" slats were painted black prior to construction, adding to the interior design.

Camillia japonica

The Field Trip

C reating a landscape takes time. You need time for the professional designer and the client to get to know one another's tastes and ways, as well as time to develop ideas and search out materials. You also need time to listen, learn and let a concept germinate, as it pushes its way out of the soil and bursts into bloom.

During this time, the client is up front, shoving the wheelbarrow, while the designer guides the process in the right direction.

I learned about the concept of time in relation to plants (or almost anything else, for that matter) early in my career. I owned a quaint little garden center, Queen Ann Nursery in Hingham, Massachusetts. When Old Man Winter withered the blooms on the vine, we would shut down and get ready for the Christmas trade, clearing off the wide shelves of prosaic things

This full parterre consists of annuals planted very closely to form color groupings separated by hedges of formal or informal patterns. The formality comes from the herringbone brick walks and raised brick edging in "soldier" form. The outside hedging plants are Myrsine africana and the inside hedge is Euonymus Microphylla "Silver King." The inside lawn, planted with Kentucky bluegrass, is on a 20' diameter. There are two entrance gates, one from the street and one from the drive entrance (See pages 24 and 27). The courtyard walls are European style with pyramid coping.

❶

and decorating them with Della Robbia wreaths and festoons made of pine boughs and cones. They gave off a fresh woodsy scent to further entice shoppers whose spirits were already on a holiday high. Hopefully, it would lead them out to the yard, where our Christmas trees, cut Fir and Scots pine, were displayed. We would hang back and wait while the buyers looked around. When we sensed some family tension in the air, I would enter the scene and offer to help.

The customer would say something like, "We want a tree about six to seven feet high that's nice and round and bushy. What do you have?"

I would show them good examples, but they hardly ever were what the customer had in mind. So, I would leave them to make their own selection and continue to help someone else. Moments later, they would emerge, all smiles, with a tree that was one-sided and so open you could throw a cat through it.

After a season or two of this, it finally got though to me that when asked what they want, people are rarely able to tell you right off. I learned that the more time I spent with them, the better the result. Ever since, I have paid much more attention to what was being said and **how** it is said, gaining a deeper

A sculptured nymph has a water flow at the top of the rings making great bath area for the birdies.
"Fairy Window" by Lester Harris

❷

23

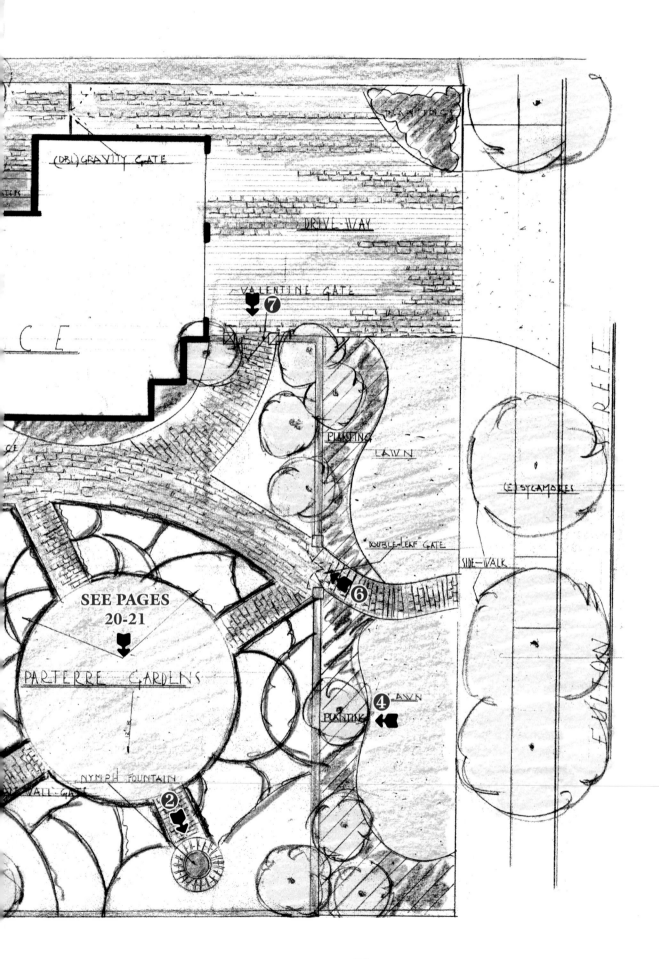

(DBL) GRAVITY GATE

DRIVE-WAY

VALENTINE GATE ⑦

PLANTING

LAWN

PLANTING

(E) SYCAMORES

DOUBLE-LEAF GATE

⑥

SIDE-WALK

SEE PAGES
20-21

PARTERRE GARDENS

④ LAWN

PLANTING ⏪

NYMPH FOUNTAIN

WALL GATE

②

STREET

FULTON

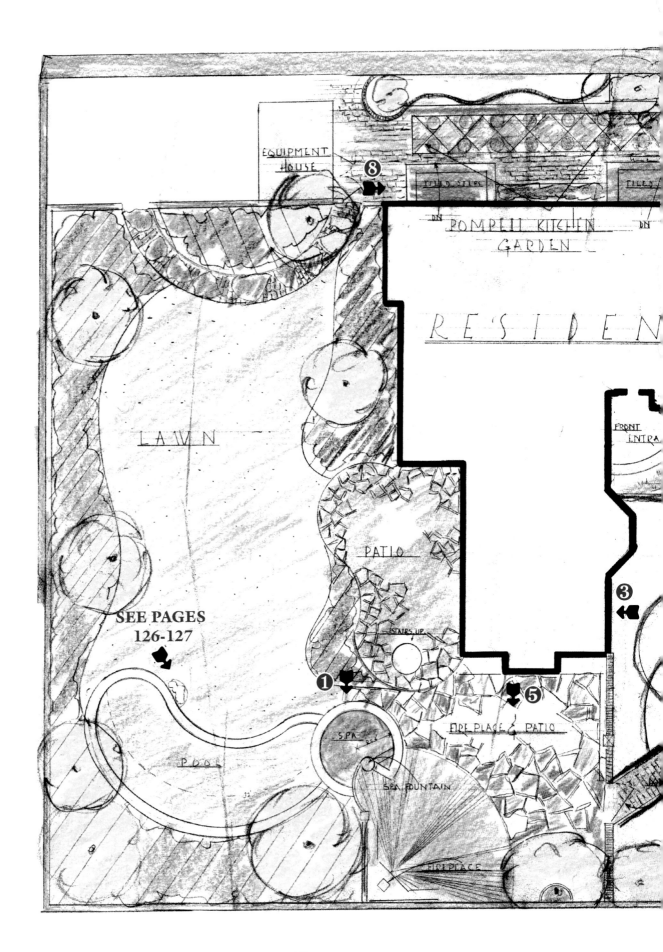

EQUIPMENT
HOUSE

⑧

TILED STEPS

TILED

DN POMPEII KITCHEN DN
GARDEN

RESIDEN

FRONT
ENTRA

LAWN

③

PATIO

STAIRS UP

**SEE PAGES
126-127**

①

⑤

FIRE PLACE PATIO

SPA

POOL

SPA FOUNTAIN

FIREPLACE

The stone terrace is made of different colored stones set on a concrete base. Areas were kept open during the concrete pour to allow for small rock-type plants to integrate the stone area. A half-circle of brick emphasizes a seating area near the fireplace and adjacent spa. **❺**

This garden entrance gate creaks a "come in" feeling. **❻**

Through another large wooden gate is a **8** garden/living space right outside the kitchen, affording complete privacy for breakfast, lunch or dinner at night with special lighting. Adjacent to a French stone mosaic floor is a slightly elevated serpentine wall, planted with aromatic herbs.

Gate designed on Valentine's day!! **7**

Within this Parterre garden is a Forsythia (spectabilis) espaliered on the front wall of the house.
This is one of the earliest Spring flowers and is very hardy, coming back year after year. ❸

A pleasant garden combination of Pachysandra terminalis is mixed with European white Birch trees. ❹

28

An entrance which exudes in style.

insight into my clients as the design process moved along.

For example, when developing a plant list, instead of imposing my own taste, I take my clients to a nursery where they feast their eyes and sharpen their senses with regards to fragrance, texture and the sound of the wind rustling through the leaves. We sometimes even taste a flower or two. All this creates a special bond between the client and designer and brings out the artistic sense in both.

Some design meetings take place at a nursery; others at stoneyards, lumberyards or simply at home. Even so, I have noted a certain reticence on the part of men to partner up and join the fun. But partnership is what it is all about and, inevitably, some cagey banter goes a long way in getting the whole family to participate. 🌺

"THIS COUPLE OWN AND OPERATE A PERIOD ANTIQUE FURNITURE BUSINESS. They travel extensively to find the better pieces for clientele willing to regard furniture as an investment as well as its purposeful use. With this in mind, I felt a need to heist up my britches another notch or two to meet their level of knowledge and exceed it artistically.

Their house had traditional overtones of New England clapboard with a roof slant of Gambrel design. The house paint was in grey tones with a Williamsburg blue trim. They had three younger children, so certain rooms displayed a type of use as needed. The living room was quite formal, while the kitchen and adjacent rooms were humanly in use. The front landscaping approach therefore was to reflect this more formal part of their personalities, as well as accommodate the terrain restrictions consisting of an upward sloping lot toward the front door.

The back yard design, an area small in space, represented their attitude after coming home from work, yet, organized enough to have it be a part of their entertaining area .

The front area was developed by using the "organizing circle" entrance scheme. One entered from the parking area to this large brick area of different shades which was fronted on the right side by a 3' high retaining wall. The retaining wall was topped by a painted, little post and rail fence with mushroom type cap finials on each post. The entrance area then proceeded into a 3' wide brick walk, chinked with moss, and up some stairs which followed the curving brick wall until eventually the steps and wall met at the same grade at the front door. The retaining wall had another purpose of developing another raised and level lawn terrace which were at the same level as the front entrance steps. This area was designed into formal elements which are delineated by boxwood hedges. The hedges outlined small planting areas for annuals and roses. All this area was quite admired from the different views inside the house.

*Although these plantings were completed in 1982,
the original design is still flowering and flourishing.*

A colonial-type entrance, a raised lawn and flower beds are part of the view from the kitchen bow window. The entrance to the curved walk is brick set on fines (See page 30). Some bricks have been removed to make room for mosses or other small plants. The fence surround is done with joinery (no nails or screws) and is completely removable for maintenance if necessary.

This rear deck consists of 2"x12" redwood planks of equal length. They are sawed diagonally from one end to the opposite end, thus leaving a "tail" or a pointed end piece. These "tails" were then placed together on the deck structure giving the deck a fan-type form.

The casual front entrance walk uses large pieces of slate flagstone plopped into the cement pour before it hardens. The cement has been colored brown.

"*THIS IS A TYPICAL NEW ENGLAND RANCH STYLE HOUSE. All work was concentrated on the front foundation area. The design called for removing all the old growth as well as an old Cottonwood tree (Poplar) whose roots were invasive. The client wanted a small area for herbs, cutting flowers and a few veggies. The process was to remove the original walk of straight concrete and then to produce a long horizontal line which when viewing the house from the street, would expand the dominate horizontal architectural lines of the residence. This line was accomplished by a ranch-style fence of two rails (6"x6" posts and 2"x8" rails) stretching from the side property line and riding all the way to the house el. When the fence came up to a point opposite the house, the fence was then incorporated into a dry stone wall. The wall was the encompassing or enclosure factor for segregating the front lawn area into another small area closer to the entrance but not visible until one approached the gate to enter this area. Inside this wall were the gardens which were separated by two formal brick walk ways running at opposing angles. From this area one then approached the front door.*

Thus, coming up the walk from the street, one would walk through a very informal exposed concrete and stone pathway of birches and sea pinks (Armeria) up to and through a gated area which was more formal, and thence into the house interior which was quite formal. The front walk was made by pouring brown colored concrete into the forms already laid out. After raking this mix to a reasonable smooth grade, the stones were then squeezed into the concrete mix before it set. The same stones were used in the wall. After the stones were set into the mix, we then water-blasted the cement mix from the top of the concrete surface to expose an irregular surface. We always color all concrete no matter for what purpose, unless it is to be used as an underlayment for support".

An octagonal raised fountain sits on a floor of random rectangular bluestone with 6" x 6" beam dividers. The inside fountain surfaces are set with very small and intricate pieces of Venetian tile and the top surface design was contributed by the family, one person per panel.

A formal patterned design for a front entrance bow window uses African box (Myrsine africaniensis) as the outside hedge, Teucrium germander as the inside hedge and Artemisia "Powis Castle" for the filler.

How do you make a house appear to be distant? Design a neat and narrow walk to the front door, make it a red one and set some brick edging an inch to an inch and a half higher in "sailor" style (See below). A little fan shaped design flourishes at the street end, indicating a step up to a small arbor with a climbing rose. Finally, plant a small 9" to 12" inch hedge of dwarf boxwood on both sides, from the street to the door.

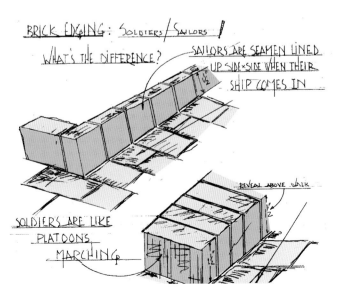

BRICK EDGING: SOLDIERS / SAILORS !
WHAT'S THE DIFFERENCE?
SAILORS ARE SEAMEN LINED UP SIDE × SIDE WHEN THEIR SHIP COMES IN
REVEAL ABOVE WALK
SOLDIERS ARE LIKE PLATOONS MARCHING

A waterfall of substance is shown flowing into a large pool with a grotto. Several different water courses of variable strengths allow a variant view from almost any angle. The plantings are black pines (Pinus thunbergia), rock and creeping mosses and other rock plants such as Cotoneaster (Lowfast), Ceonothus (Yankee point), Artemisia (Powis Castle), Chaenomeles (Quince Apple Blossom) and various mosses used for color and foliage. A small trail leads around and through the water troughs, starting from the upper spa area.

Access to the spa is hidden in back of the waterfall (See above) providing privacy and space.

A visual setback is extended from the front entrance to the doorway. A different color grout is used with the Bluestone. Two opposing Acer palmatum (15 gallon) are tied together at the top to form a growing arch.

A Moorish style stone entrance includes a mosaic fountain. The 12"x12" stones are in mottled colors ranging from green to a rust patina. The joints are widened and filled with 1"x3" jade green tiles. Sea Pinks (Armeria maritime) are massed among the Birch clusters and the foreground hedging is Taxus hatfieldii and Japanese Yew. The tall hedge in the background is Thuja occidentalis pyramidalis. The penetration type entrance courtyard uses a reddish-brown 3/8" crushed stone.

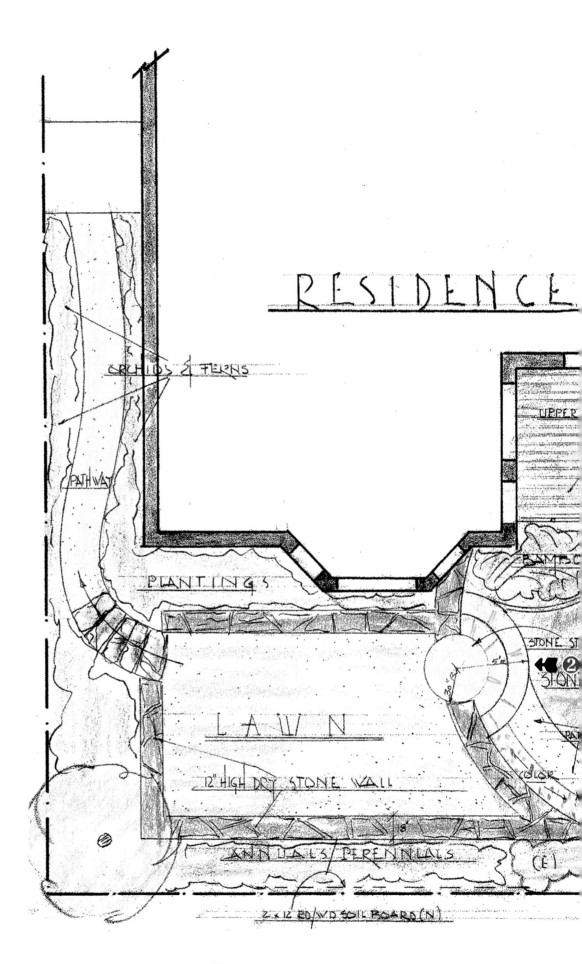

RESIDENCE

UPPER

ORCHIDS & FERNS

PATHWAY

PLANTINGS

BAMBOO

STONE ST

STON

LAWN

12" HIGH DRY STONE WALL

ANNUALS/ PERENNIALS

2 x 12 RD/WD SOIL BOARD (N)

See page pages 156-157 for an upstairs view of this stairway.

❸

42

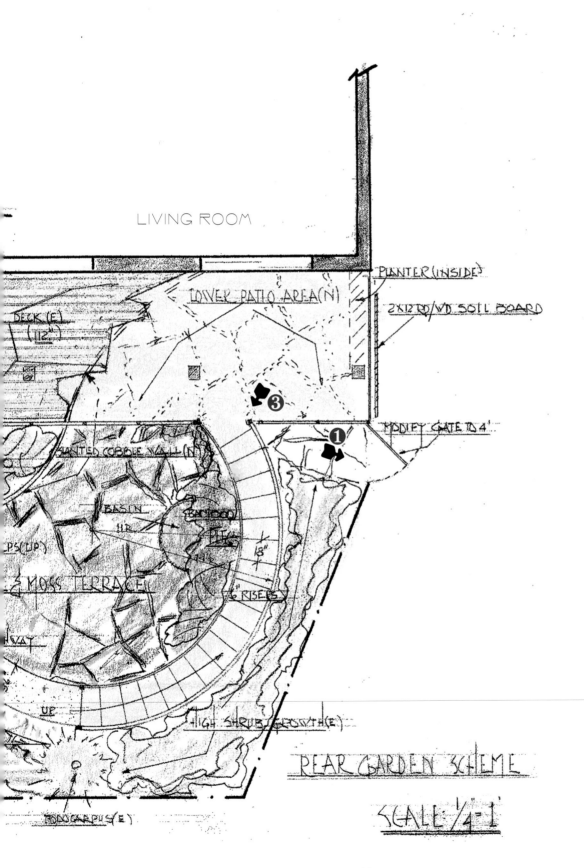

LIVING ROOM

PLANTER (INSIDE)

LOWER PATIO AREA (N)

2×12 RD/WD SOIL BOARD

DECK (E)
(112")

③

①

MODIFY GATE TO 4'

PLANTED COBBLE WALL (N)

BASIN

1 R.

BAMBOO
PIPE

18"

6" RISERS

PS (UP)

3 MOSS TERRACE (

VAT

UP

HIGH SHRUB GROWTH (E)

REAR GARDEN SCHEME

SCALE: ¼"=1'

PODOCARPUS (E)

PLEASE LIFT →

②

In this design entry to the back area is from the upper living room deck . The original access was through the lower level master bedroom, or outside between the garage and property line, neither being a good option. It was decided to use the upper balcony and gain access by way of building a stairway with a close radius. The ironwork was fabricated and brought in by crane.

As the plan indicates, there are two areas, a formal and informal. The former was raised 24" with steps down to the lower flagstone patio which is right off the master bedroom access. The plantings here were essentially existing, but an addition of bamboo, used as a filler under the staircase, worked quite well. The local birds loved it to the delight of the owners.

The formal area is used for lawn parties and small functions . Of course, the English Cottage garden flower beds give much color, scent, and cut flowers the owner may need for the house and entertaining. An outside fence post and gate with a "haines" (Remember the old horse days?) and hanging pot of flowers add a unique touch.

①

A brick pathway leads to a formal living room terrace. The brick pattern allows the open joints to be filled with Irish moss. These joints are prominent enough for direction, especially when the perennial beds are in full growth.

This quiet section of water is situated right next to a front entrance and accommodates the mood of the passerby from reflective to adventurous.

The photographs on these two pages, are of a backyard measuring about 50' x 50'. This small area has a list of many uses, yet it has the feeling of a much larger area with careful assignment of color to paved areas (lighter) and keeping brick areas on a running bond type of design. The plantings caress the corners and nothing is overdone.

47

English Ivy swags line this lovely driveway entrance.

Formal gardens and a magnificient flowering Dogwood with beds of Tulips invite guest to this quaint house.

A petite yard provides for intimate dining or an elegant luncheon for six. Fragrances abound in this bi-level entertaining area.

Wisteria vines enclose this balcony/bedroom area.

Stairs spiral down from the upper master bedroom balcony to a spa and garden seating space.

Magnelia stellata

A Head Start on Garden Design

I n my first book, *Chadwick on Individualized Landscaping*, there is great emphasis put on getting to know the client. If you take the trouble to do that, once the garden is completed, you can compare it with that knowledge and much of what you see in the design should be a personal reflection of the person for whom it was designed.

You should be able to learn your clients' preferences and lifestyle without their being consciously involved in the process through the interpretation of conversation, attention to words and facial expressions. It takes some time but can be accomplished over the entire space of putting together all aspects of the design, especially during the actual construction phases.

These phases should not necessarily be accomplished in a linear manner; first one thing, then another, then the next. One should take the trouble to understand the client on a steady but varied timetable by arranging different kinds of field trips and interweaving past and present conversations. It is an ongoing therapy session of sorts and, like a good therapist, you should not try to be the principal but the guide.

A preliminary design sketch is useful for establishing the parameters and needs, both aesthetically and economically. This first sketch merely establishes the design goals (where the drives, walks, etc. will be placed) and should not be driven by financial considerations. There will be plenty of time for that once the designer begins to innovate and implement the choices. In the beginning, it is simply enough to open the lines of communication.

Over time, you should be able to ascertain the particular psychological characteristics of the client by creating conversations and listening carefully. What is heard may be introduced into the design and transformed into an environmental emotion. Patience, guidance and the bringing of all one's expertise to defining a solution constitutes landscape garden therapy at its finest. 🌰

*This "design access"
to a public ramp helps
<u>alert</u> handicap to
change of grade*

A stock brokerage, jeweler and an ice cream parlor occupy this multi-business area. A central open space allows shoppers or visitors to pause and relax. An iron railing takes up minimal space with 1/4" spindles spaced 3" apart. A water fountain is located on the curved back wall.

This property line consists of a serpentine
wall which is great for the neighbors as well

... creating a nice way to top off the common property line.

This clear-view gate, delicate against the background, provides an unobsturcted view .

Some bricks of the parking area are removed for a plant.

Shown here
is one of the
nicest ways
to end a wall.
Originally there
was to be a
birdbath in this
space but too
many other
four legged
furry fellows
also thought
it a nice idea.
Swish, Swish.

58

Here you can enjoy an infinity walk to the sea, joined with colorful slate bending slightly to the left.

59

Sometimes a driveway must be disguised to look less like a parking lot. This effect uses a dominant front door entrance path, while offering a utilitarian and attractive area for cars. There are four types of bricks and brick placements in this driveway .

A ranch-style house and a long low wall accentuate the horizontal axis of the house. Balance is achieved for the foreground of Festuca glauca (Blue fescue grass) planted under a cluster of European White Birch within a lawn area.

A Japanese out building with shoji screens was built joinery style.

61

From a distance the low horizontal dry stone wall appears part of the foundation. This is done to pull together the various elevations of the house. Looking at it close up, the wall becomes another factor in that of a retaining wall with more lawn and some low plantings. The driveway is a Penetration type construction (See page 135-136).

"*THIS HOUSE IS SITED ON ONE OF THE LOVELIEST LOTS I HAVE SEEN. Huge old redwoods tower over the winding entrance road and over the residence as well. I wondered when I first met the owner why or what he needed. One of the prominent motives for the new landscaping resulted from an incident two years previous when their younger daughter was practicing her piano lesson. It was during a windstorm when one of the limbs from a Redwood tree broke from its source and came crashing through the roof and ended up at her side! Apparently the trauma of this caused so much discomfort that the intent was to sell the property. Thus, he felt that something special was needed to further enhance the main perspective of the estate. The changes were essentially twofold: one was to create a new vehicular area for turning around and yet be kept away from the garaging area; the other was the focal point and balancing of the architecture to the main entrance. These were accomplished by beginning at the road entrance and smoothing out the curved roadway into a central location. At the central location a large circular turnaround was established. This was visually connected at once to the main entrance walk. Thence, the main entrance walk was elaborated upon by a low dry stone wall which covered the entire foundation of the residence and in the center of which were the stepping transitions to the front door. This wall helped blend out all the irregular shapes and images of the building.*

In back of this wall on a higher elevation, yet not higher than the wall itself, was a lawn area which had much value in color and texture. Around the house foundation were planted Azaleas and other broadleaf evergreens, enough to form a continuous mass of dark greens. In the front of the wall were the lawn areas, split by the entrance walk of mortared chocolate flagstone with a green grout. The pool area was somewhat visible from the turnaround. Not until one walked further to the side of the house toward the garage or, from the house itself, could one appreciate the fine view of its setting. The pool had to be fully viewed from their kitchen and family rooms for safety reasons. Another large lawn area open to the sun was created on the opposite side of the house near the bedrooms, used for recreational purposes.

The entrance road and all the boundary areas from it were planted with very large Rhododendrons, Dogwoods and Flowering Crabs. In addition other plantings were intermixed such as many ferns, azaleas, and potentillas. Around the rear of the house a stone pathway was placed and entirely planted with Irish moss. On the sides of this pathway were planted more of the above types of flowering evergreens and trees which took advantage of the large amount of glass along that side of the house for viewing from within. The roadway was surfaced with a small brown crushed stone which gave the final touch and feeling of impeccable participation."

"THEY WERE ON THE LAST LEG OF IMPROVING THEIR HOUSE with a lovely library and sitting room wing which extended into the rear landscape.

About thirty huge pine trees, 50' high, were growing along the back side of their property and since there was only a distance of 30' from the house to these trees, the yard was always in the dark. Trees were planted because this lot looks upward to houses along their boundary. Privacy was needed at the time but now it was too much. They owned a small hothouse which they liked to use for growing small seeds and annuals. She enjoyed the yard immensely.

My suggestions first centered on the privacy, for which I designed a large tilted Arbor to replace all of the trees. This Arbor was designed to be 8' in height at its highest altitude and 5' from the grade level at its lowest point. It was made in two uneven sections and planted with five or six different types of flowering vines, some of which were evergreen. In a year or two the vines would amass growth enough to not only block out the neighbor's view but provide some fine blossoms and fragrances as well.

The center attraction was a brick patio which was visually connected to their new wing. From this addition one stepped out through a French door opening to two semicircular steps and onto the brick area. This pattern of brick was concentric at first beginning from an old city street light and thence the circles changed in radii becoming larger as the terrace widened. One type of brick was used as they felt several types of brick would be too busy.

From this terrace one followed a small brick pathway around the wing to the sideyard where the hothouse was situated on a brick platform, all clean and organized which suited them well. She went mad with flowers everywhere and the yard looked quite happy."

One of the most fun projects I have done is this little entrance court to an upstairs front door. This is all the client had to use for a little garden therapy. So a large circle envelopes the front step, part of the gate entrance, and the door to a garage! The potting area is where it should be, an espaliered apple is fixed to the right wall of the garage, and a lazy English Ivy (Hedera), is about to run itself up the wire which is attached to the step casing, which indicates, "follow me".

The fountain in this scene is so minimal one has to really wonder from where the sound comes. It helps the design if one looks around.

"THE FRONT ENTRANCE OF THIS TOWNHOUSE CONSISTED ONLY OF A LANDING AND FRONT DOOR". The rearyard measured about 16'x25' with a side area of about 6'x30' which connected to the front landing door. Most of the land was flat, except the front landing was elevated about 5' from the side and rear areas.

Requirements included a spa within an existing small deck area which was placed adjacent to their livingroom door and in an el shape to their bedroom door. The deck was also elevated about 5' above the backyard. She loved to putter and wished something easy to manage, reminding her of "Back East" informal with traditional motifs.

The front entrance concrete pad was removed and replaced with a brick on fines circular pattern with an espaliered Wisteria running up alongside the stair railing right to the front door. On the wall to the left on the house side, we espaliered a Granny Smith apple tree on six-armed style which took up some bare space as well and helped the visual form in entering the area. As one arrived on the landing a gate was part of the wall which proceeded to a long boardwalk to the rearyard area. Surrounding this boardwalk was a tall hedge of evergreens (Arborvitae) nicely trimmed. The view was somewhat alleé like. The walk along this 3' wide wood path leads to the left opening to the spa deck and straight ahead it came to a set of stairs leading down to the garden. In the garden area was a rectangular wall of dry stone which was about 18" high and as wide. Centered in the wall along the back of the property was a sunken fountain. The water came through a stone cap and puddled back into a basin beneath. Around all sides in back of this wall were flowers, small trees for shade and vines on the fencing. The terrace itself was of brick placed on fines in a running bond fashion. Another garden walk rising to the spa deck area was on the opposite end of the terrace area, made up of washed river rock and chinked with moss. Lighting gave a special nighttime effect."

*One day
I returned
to check
on this
garden.
Behold, a
bear was
protecting
the roses
inside!*

Tritorme

Sight Unseen

Having had the rare opportunity of designing a garden for a friend who could not see, I can tell you that, faced with this kind of challenge, all sorts of inventions come to mind. Do you try to find a school for the blind and ask for help? How do you translate color for the sightless and does it really matter? If you draw a design, should it be in Braille with post notes at walking intervals describing garden elements or just a smooth walking surface with a low elevation bar for leg guidance?

People who cannot see or who only have some peripheral vision and have lived with this disability for a time are usually super-sensitive to what is going on around them. Most seek educational and practical therapy at an institution for their support needs and, after a while probably exceed normally sighted people in the ability to manipulate their environment. The development of one's visceral senses, (those of touch, smell, taste and sound), is highly motivated when vision is lost or impaired. Trying to regulate between the conditions of no first-hand knowledge on the part of the designer and all kinds of adaptability for the blind client can be a difficult task.

Total immersion seems to be the best solution and, before long, a role reversal should ensue. If you think that a better garden can be had with the eyes closed, your subjectivity will leap to unknown heights. After that happens, over a set of experiences, your objectivity will catch up and both the right and left sides of your brain will be performing quite efficiently. In my own particular experience, I had always been told to "open my eyes and see the world" but, in this instance, rather like Christopher Columbus, I discovered a whole new world when I closed them.

Of course it is necessary to get some background from a professional source and, to that end, I worked with the Perkins Institute for the Blind and the Carroll Center for the Blind, located, respectively, in Watertown and Newton Centre, Massachusetts. I did not take any formal lessons but found a wealth of information through discussion and literature at both sites. These institutions each have a great deal

ALERT!!! At once your foot feels a difference and down your eyes go, or, for those who are sight impaired, slow or stop to check the walk pavement.

of diversity in teaching and place much emphasis on practice for living. The Perkins Institute even has a special building and gardens devoted to garden therapy.

The first step in the garden design process is total immersion for both subjects right on the area to be planned. Arm in arm, both parties should start at a prescribed spot, such as the back door of the client's home. From there, your client starts to walk in areas to be devoted to lawn, garden, walkways, etc. At the same time he or she is guiding the trail, you, the designer, must be asking questions such as: "What about cooking herbs?" "Tall flowers vs. small ones?" "Fountains or bench for relaxing?" You should also ask about what kind of directional guidance to use and when or how to feel approaching objects and walkways.

Before construction begins, the gardens should be outlined with string indicating directions and "observing areas," especially if there is a view (in the particular case we are discussing, it was Cape Cod Bay to the east). During construction, frequent meetings should be arranged to iron out the practicalities. By the time completion is near, the designer with eyes

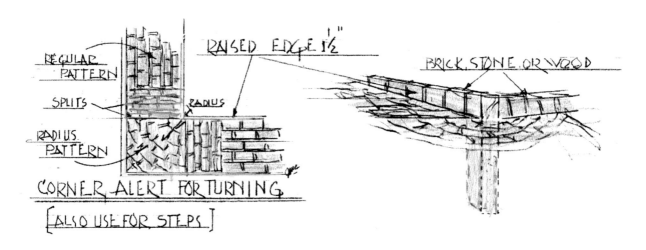

REGULAR PATTERN

SPLITS

RADIUS PATTERN

RAISED EDGE 1½"

RADIUS

BRICK, STONE, OR WOOD

CORNER ALERT FOR TURNING

[ALSO USE FOR STEPS]

closed, could interchange with the client. What really happens is that all one's sensitivities develop to a high degree when eyesight is taken away. If you want to take your other four visceral senses on a holiday, close your eyes!

Upon the conclusion of this field trip, I then make up the plant list and, gauging from what I have observed of the client's reaction to the stimulation of their senses, the rest of the work is easy. I can feel assured in finishing a planting list based on the client's actual sense of need.

The arrangement and artistic placement of the actual material is left up to me. For the client, it is the best of all possible worlds. They have been through the process and made their wishes known according to their particular desires and way of life. The choice has been theirs and the work will be mine. ✿

*It doesn't depend on how **you** arrange the landscape, it's how the landscape will be arranged in the client's mind.*

An original California Pepper Tree (Schinus molle) surrounded by a dry laid stone wall for quiet and shady lounging. A fantastic graceful tree for warm weather areas.

Dry stone wall with Irish moss.

Leave No Stone Unturned

After building many stone walls and a lot of stone layment walks and patios over the years, one thing becomes clear about this material (besides the need for a new pair of knees). Stone is always beautiful, no matter which side is up.

Having lived in California and New England for a long time, I think I've seen it all because most of the stone yards, especially in northern California, import from all over the world. Traveling around the various residential areas in this region affords the experience of an International stone exposition. This is guaranteed to give variety, but less likely to establish any kind of consistent tradition.

Most of the stone walls I have put together are "dry", that is they have no footing or mortar between the stone layments. This might lead one to fear that they might fall down or, if higher than 5', actually fall over. Rest easy. If there is anything more permanent than Fort Knox, it is a dry stone wall.

This way of wall building first came about in Continental Europe and Asia, making its way here with the Pilgrims. Stone material, such as huge granite slabs, originally was used for building foundations, gristmills, mill spools and even as ballast for the ships. It also was fashioned into 7' sandstone rounds that were used for grinding swords and knives.

When the settlers began to farm the land, so much clearing of the rocks and boulders was required that, when piled up, the cleared debris became a boundary wall or a stone fence. After a generation or two, the farmers began to straighten the stones out by stacking them in place. This not only made the fence more attractive but allowed the cows to look over, brightening up their day as well.

As time progressed, the walls became more intricate and turned into works of art in and of themselves. The major reason there was no foundation under them was because of the heaving of the ground with the winter frosts. When spring came, the walls settled down to their normal grade, none the worse for wear. Up and down, year after year, the walls stood, creating a home for birds, chipmunks, snakes and a host of other woodland folk. I don't know of any concrete walls that could last that long and help accommodate creatures of the wild at the same time.

Building a stone wall is an art form. Observing a skilled mason place the stones as if each stone was a personal friend, kind of half-whistling to himself as he ponders the fit, is a very companionable business. Watching a wall like this being built is like observing a dog with his bone. Leave him alone until it's done.

In case you were wondering what else goes into the wall, there also is what is termed "chinks," small chips of stone, sand or gravel mixture (gray fines or stone dust). This helps with the binding and leveling. That's all there is to it. Just put it together and stand back. I promise you, the wall will stand there as long as you do, and even longer. ✻

Precision stacking of this variety of stone creates a very strict formality and is usually designed for with entrances, driveways or enclosures to formal gardens. Very effective.

"THIS PROJECT WAS DONE PRIOR TO MY WORLD TRIP.

I mention this because it seemed to mark a sense of style or mood change from the more traditionally correct Eastern balance to the more Asian which shows more interest in emotional interpretation.

The lot size was angular, flat and in a section of the San Francisco Bay Area which was more traditional and reserved, quite settled compared to other nearby areas. These clients were quite refined, intelligent and able to be stretched to the limit as far as innovation was concerned. She was also very talented in designing interior spaces.

The design began with the cobblestone driveway and court-yard. The cobbles were found in Stockton, California, stockpiled from different localities and in every conceivable color. They were placed on a sand base with sand joints. Some were replaced with bricks which emulate the house facade and existing brick wing wall. The

This courtyard is good for posing your expensive antique car. The majority of the surface is varied colored cobblestone set upon a coarse sand bed, with joints of about one or more inches. These joints are filled with the same course sand or with concrete.

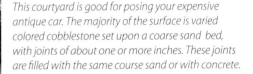

pool area was tied to a three-sided open porch area done with a classic touch. Its pavement was brick mosaic in varying sized arcs. A double rollock edge dramatizes a Delphi look. The pool was coped with one row of bricks with an edging of brick that was open spaced for water let out. This also modeled a repetition of the classic mold. Plant-ings were left until the last event, in order to ascertain the best color background for summer and winter. The clients entertained much, and she always kept potted plants in abundance. The kitchen patio was quite secluded and charming in its quiet and useful way. They used this for reading in the morning and just to admire creating a nice juxtaposition of materials in a small space."

73

"AFTER A DAY'S WORTH OF SHOWING THEM *some of my previous works, the clients wrote me a check while in the car,*
quite convinced. The site area was actually quite small considering all the ideas and needs thrown into it. Originally
an existing patio was separated by some wild bamboo hiding a small propagating 15' x 30' greenhouse. The foundation for
this became the "pivot" idea for the mode of construction, as the design for the Pagoda centered on this item.

The design philosophy appeared rather quickly in that the client's work ethic required him to reverse his stress standard

after leaving the high energy stock exchange. Her requirements were stated as being subordinate and to use the area as only
a play time. Her usual pastime was occupied by their horses and training programs elsewhere on the site. I had just returned
from a world tour and fresh ideas had replaced old boundaries of habits, (Remember Walter Pater's dictum, 'failure is to form
habits'?). Therefore the Zen philosophy, using the power of natural resources to restore and question our breadth of thoughts
seemed a most appropriate design initiative.

The main requirements were a swimming pool, small entertainment areas and a place to contemplate.

The use of red brick and grey stone softened by green kept a dominant sense of control and allowed capitulation to rule

Interpretation

The Torii Gate, a portal for Shinto religion, is based upon entering a meditative and enlightenment garden for intuitive thought and practice. This gate is made with two horizontal cross pieces, the top piece is redwood and will warp upward with sun action. This would express a perch for the tori bird. The entire gate is free of all mechanics, leaving its action and manufacture clean of contrivance or human artifact. Thus, one is entering a spiritual aura of respectability and protection. The gates rotate on two pins, top and bottom, and open with only a slight press of the hands.

over balance and structure. The rule in contemplative environments is being able to make strong elements delicate and yet run the show. One becomes immersed in the singular volume of oneself and is held in control by the very fact of self appraisal using small objects of realities.

The project was on two levels about the size of a football field. The two levels, as linear and motional lines, became more fluid, arid and dramatic as one walked upstairs and looked down upon a garden and felt the difference. Many designers relate to this experience as 'creating an illusion'. The mindful sense was not to create an illusion but to extend what the mind already knows, to another reality. Here was an opportunity to take advantage of the site for this purpose.

Many of the smaller design elements came during the construction process, wherein each days entrance into the project area would give a new look to yesterdays work. Studying it for a while, I would proceed to work on the project at close hand, making the changes or not. It's the same with any hands-on artist, sculptor or painter, one must be within the framework of the "chip and cut" to sense its movement and durability.

This project was done by subcontractors doing the usual basic trades, assisted by my son, David Chadwick.

One entered the garden by gently pushing the double Torri gate doors (not hinged) and immediately viewed the upper level terrace and in the distance the Bridge and Pagoda. The brick upper terrace was laid in three patterns of influence showing the motion of the Pacific Ocean currents. Islands of green moss introduced a calming influence. As one proceeded to the Pagoda, one noticed the bridge, which was made of slatted wood slightly spaced to massage the feet. The sides of it were quite different; one was curved and one was flat. The Pagoda had shoji screens surrounding the spa which then could be private or open. The pine floor boards creaked a bit noting vulnerability. Looking out and down to the pool area, a sense of more perception was gained by the flow of the brick pattern around the pool as well as the change of blue color of the pool from that of shallow to deep. One descended down into the pool area on a set of stone steps which were protruding out of the curved and circular stone wall. Standing at the rear of the pool and looking back one could appreciate the magnitude of the environment in such a small space with all its changing colors in each season."

The Zen Garden is thought of as a Sea of Tranquility (See page 74). Different currents i.e. the brick placements lead one to an area of land or closer islands and continue on to a pensive bridge (See page 84). This is contemplative for its unbalanced nature, and spans a gorge which is constantly wrapped in fog (via mist nozzles) indicating one's indecision for change. *Why then is the bridge so narrow and unbalanced with a floor of wood spaces to view the precipitous depths below? Is the seat necessary to sit upon or should one cling to the high rail for relief? Where does one move when the water beckons?*

The Water Retreat and the Pagoda with its island refuge behind the Shoji screens beckon. Walk to it across the sometimes moaning pegged boards. The screens will not move by the hand. Only by swiping the feet across the channeled grooves will they move with balanced movement. Then, with an easy motion one may slide into the deep and hot spa water. Its thermal essence's a serene mental experience offering possible cerebral aid to the questions and answers thus far experienced.

Now with a pure mind for thoughts.
"We are what we think.
All that we are arises with our thoughts.
With our thoughts we make the world.
Speak or act with a pure mind and
happiness will follow you as
your shadow, unshakable."

From the *DHAMMAPADA*
(the sayings of Buddha)

A dream extended to a realty for the client.

The Pagoda is placed upon the top of a circular stone wall, its foundation walls being perpendicular on the inside, yet curved inward on the exterior (See pages 79-80). This best radiates perception of the eternal soul and its koan of enlightenment.

The answer is always in the form of a question from which one must obtain intuitive knowledge for self and body. The Torii gate protects whoever travels within for shelter and quiet contemplation.

Entering the spa, water is a condition of giving up one's own body to the weightlessness of thought and the vastness of etheral spirituality.

The construction, with few exceptions to accommodate modern building codes, of the Pagoda is all joinery, thus the sight of machine-made fasteners do not corrupt the pureness of thought. Nothing interferes with the introspection. ✤

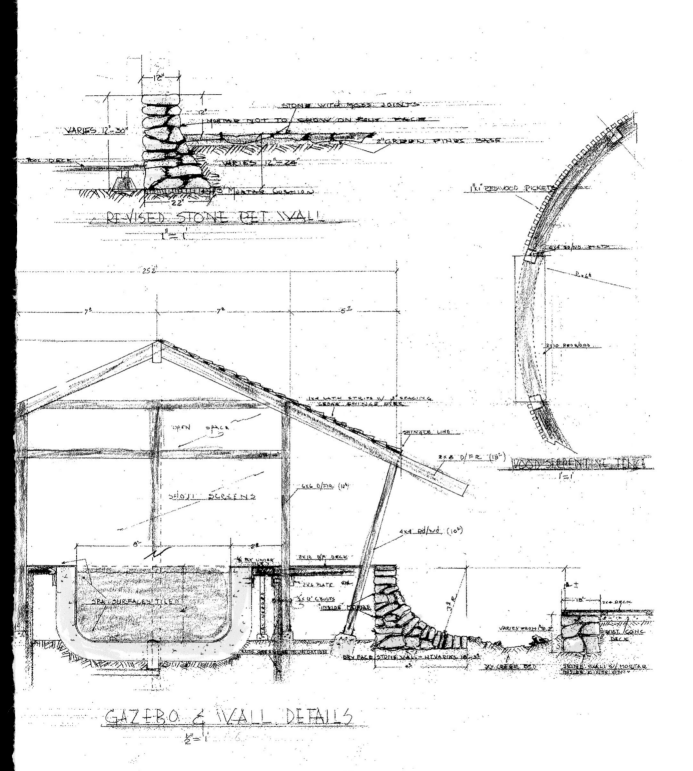

REVISED STONE RET WALL
1"=1'

WOOD SERPENTINE FENCE
1'=1'

GAZEBO & WALL DETAILS
½"=1'

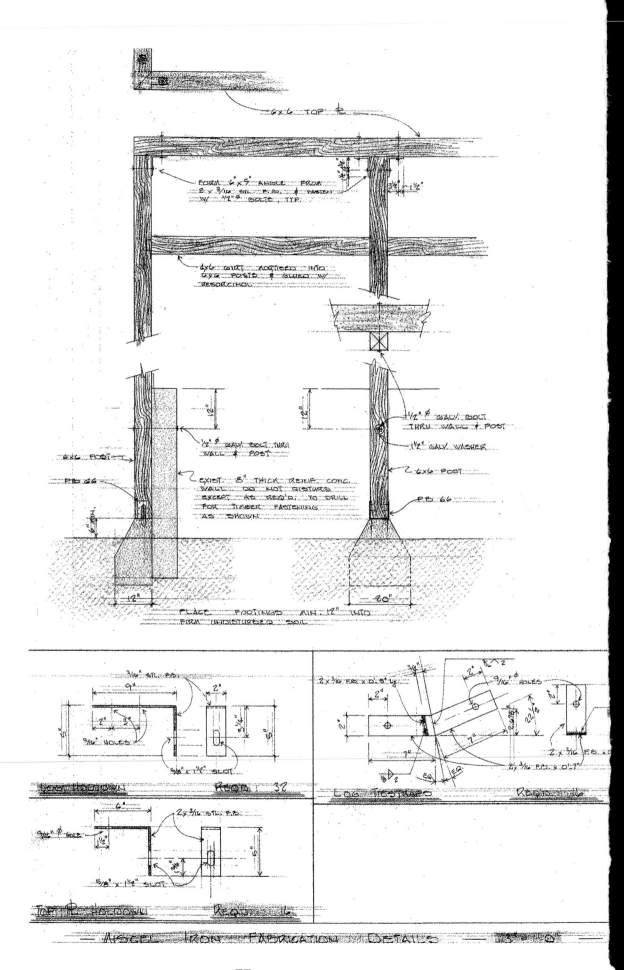

FORM 6" x 5" ANGLE FROM
2 x 3/16 STL. P.B. & FASTEN
W/ 1/2" Ø BOLTS. TYP.

6x6 GIRT NOTCHED INTO
6x6 POSTS & GLUED W/
RESORCINOL

6x6 TOP PL.

1/2" Ø GAL. BOLT THRU
WALL & POST

6x6 POST

PB 66

1/2" Ø GALV. BOLT
THRU WALL & POST

1 1/2" GALV. WASHER

2-6x6 POST

PB 66

EXIST. 8" THICK REINF. CONC.
WALL. DO NOT DISTURB
EXCEPT AS REQ'D. TO DRILL
FOR TIMBER FASTENING
AS SHOWN

12"

20"

PLACE FOOTINGS MIN. 12" INTO
FIRM UNDISTURBED SOIL

3/16" STL. P.B.

9"

2"

2"

3 1/2"

5"

9/16" HOLES

5/8" x 1 1/2" SLOT

POST HOLDOWN   REQD. 32

2 x 3/16 STL. P.B.

6"

9/16" Ø HOLE

1 1/2"

5"

5/8" x 1 1/2" SLOT

TOP PL. HOLDOWN   REQD. 16

2 x 3/16 P.B. x 0'-5 1/2"

2"

2"

2"

9/16" HOLES

7"

7"

EQ.   EQ.

2 x 3/16 P.B. x 0'-7"

LOG TIE STRAPS   REQD. 16

MISCEL. IRON FABRICATION DETAILS   1 1/2"=1'-0"

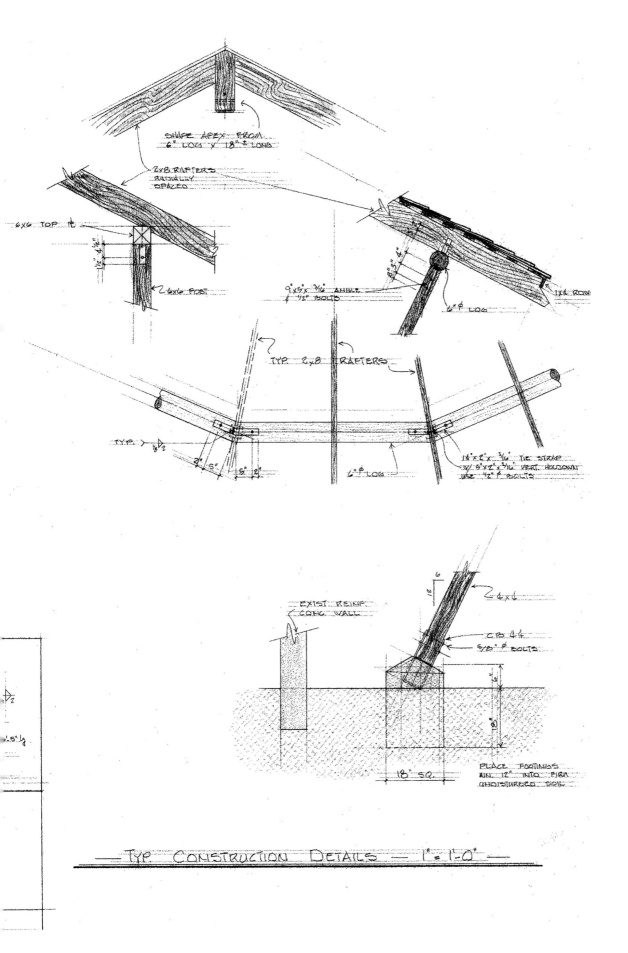

SHAPE APEX FROM
6" LOGS x 18" ± LONG

2x8 RAFTERS
RADIALLY
SPACED

6x6 TOP PL.

2 6x6 POST

9"x5"x 3/16" ANGLE
W/ 1/2" BOLTS

12"Ø LOG

1x6 ROW

TYP 2x8 RAFTERS

TYP 2x8 RAFTERS

6"Ø LOG

14"x2"x 3/16" TIE STRAP
W/ 5"x2"x 3/16" VERT. HOLDOWN
USE 1/2" Ø BOLTS

EXIST. REINF.
CONC. WALL

2 4x6

CB 44
5/8" Ø BOLTS

18" SQ.

PLACE FOOTINGS
MIN 12" INTO FIRM
UNDISTURBED SOIL

TYP. CONSTRUCTION DETAILS — 1"=1'-0"

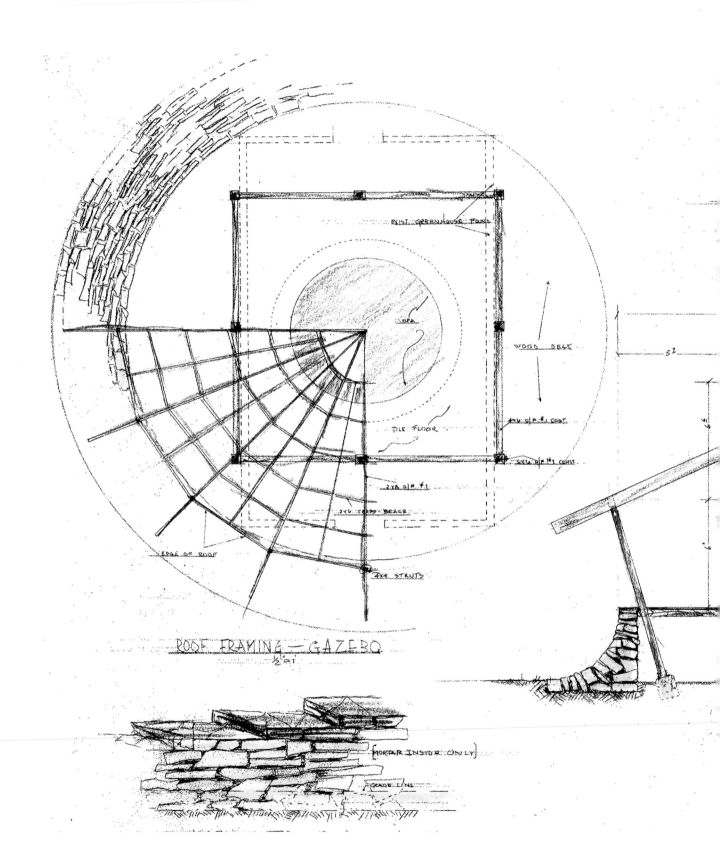

EXIST. GREENHOUSE FOUND.

OPA.

WOOD DECK

5^2

TILE FLOOR

2X6 D/F #1 CONST.

2X6 D/F #1 CONST.

2X8 D/F #1

2X6 CROSS BRACE

EDGE OF ROOF

4X4 STRUTS

ROOF FRAMING — GAZEBO
½"=1'

[MORTAR INSIDE ONLY]

GRADE LINE

The making of a Japanese Pagoda, a Zen motif, gets its use of questions for tranquility of visual contemplation .

A WORD ON "DRY" STONE WALLS

1. THEY ARE BUILT WITHOUT MORTAR
2. THEY ARE VERY STRONG AS THE ROCK IS LAID IN SUCH A WAY AS TO SUPPORT THE OTHERS AROUND IT. TEAM WORK.
3. THEY DO NOT REQUIRE A FOUNDADATION. THE OLD TIMERS DIDN'T HAVE TIME!
4. THEIR VISUAL IMAGE IS FULL OF CHARACTER AND REFINEMENT.
5. CHIPMUNKS LOVE THEM.......

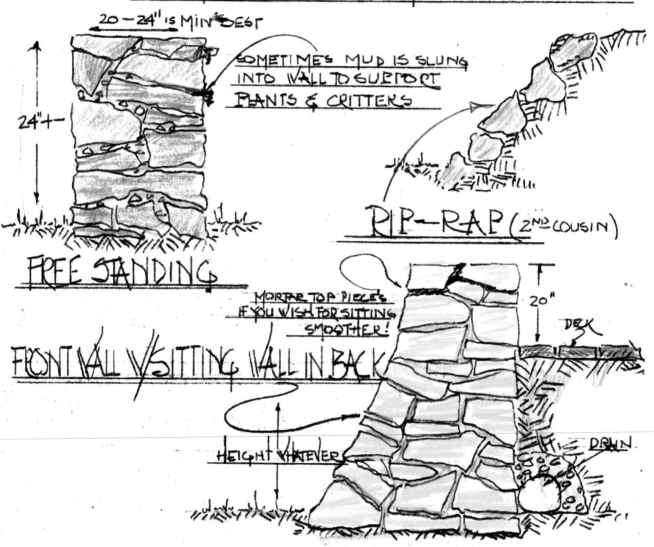

20 – 24" IS MIN BEST

24" +

SOMETIMES MUD IS SLUNG INTO WALL TO SUPPORT PLANTS & CRITTERS

RIP—RAP (2ND COUSIN)

FREE STANDING

MORTAR TOP PIECES IF YOU WISH FOR SITTING SMOOTHER!

FRONT WALL V/SITTING WALL IN BACK

T 20"

DECK

HEIGHT WHATEVER

DRAIN

*The stone steps that lead to the spa inside the
Pagoda are "laid into" the wall as it is being built.*

*The built-in steps actually drop one step below the grade. One then
must step-up to achieve a consciousness of walking and rising.*

A bridge leads to the spa from the sea of islands of tranquility and motions.

The spa area offers contemplation of the distant views along with the therapy of water movement around one's body.

Built-in steps to this 6' stonewall lead down to a lower terraced area.

On the lower pool terrace a "tea patio" is creating a perpetual area for contemplation.

The lower pool follows the flow of the fencing.

The upper entrance area depicts the Pacific Ocean emulating its currents and far flung islands.

Some designs are too perfect and just don't work! Here's one that does; a bridge from the street to the back door.
It seems the family wanted a better and shorter way from school to the kitchen pantry! We got the idea, so this is
the result, a children's own "home from schoo" bridge.

The pool is designed and approved. The pool builder, concrete contractor, masonry and tile are then selected. Every step is
discussed for original lay-out to the final dig. Many times after the pool surface is designed "on the ground"
before digging, the client and designer take a final look for changes before the excavation continues.

Seven varieties of brick are incorporated within this traffic circle and front entrance area. Set by hand on a medium/coarse sand base, the patterns are varied enough to minimize the size of the area, the lighter center pattern being the focus. A great advantage for using a porous base for the brick is to allow for percolation which absorbs rainwater into the soil. The entrance way is more concentrated with the lighter brick color and also the introduction of three courses of granite pavers nearing the house entrance better define that opening.

"THIS PROJECT, LASTING ABOUT THREE YEARS FROM START TO FINISH resulted from very thorough communication with the client. Both wished to be involved in the decision making process. Many field trips were made to view materials or objects. Many sketches were done to obtain the consensus. I really can't say that this method of decision making with the client produced the absolute best design of art, but it surely was very good. Sometimes I had wished to make a final decision for them, but they are the type to proceed dependent on the budget and a soul searching process.

The first project was to design and build the formal courtyard entrance which was attached to the front door entrance. This large paved area of brick on fines was laid out as a circle with varying patterns of brick, some flat, side-up, etc., using

88

This Spanish quadra-loop planter doubles as planter and sitting wall. The Chinese stone terrace of mixed colors serve as an outside entertainment area off the main living room.

five different kinds of brick and brick colors. Near the outside rim of this circle was a layer of 9"x9" Chinese cut granite stone. This stone began to be picked up once again in the patterns proceeding to the front entrance. As one approached the front entrance one took two 4" steps, with the leading edges smoothing the visual demand for detail. Since the front door was facing 90 degrees away from the direction of entry (five radii in each turning circle) enacting a subliminal desire to turn in the direction of the door. The door pattern of slivers is set in concrete.

The formal living room garden and terrace was made up of Chinese Jade stone mixed with 20% black to offer relief and character. All grout in this pavement was green to enhance the color of the stone. A sitting wall surrounds the birch tree growth

A wrap-around decking serves as a tennis gallery for the sunken tennis court.

in the center of the terrace. The wall was done in Moorish taste, a very smooth white plaster, pleasing to touch and sit upon.

The encompassing 6' high garden wall of a single brick width was laid out on a 6' radius which was a perfect serpentine wall ratio. The mortar here was colored with yellow and green to liven the materials. Espalier work was done on spots of the wall, Belgian patterns of crossing shrubs of Forsythia and Plumbago. An art deco gate design then took one to the tennis court. The design on this gate was made up of round circles the size of tennis balls.

The tennis court was sunken, giving it a feeling of smallness, surrounded by a one foot stone wall. Though there was a high fencing around this court, it appeared small and inconsequential.

A large slate patio extends from the house foundation to the edge of the pool.
The steps into the pool are of the same material and offer a clear, larger visual area.

The rear living spaces, on the following page, are meant to be enjoyed quite freely, whereas the other side of the house is more for adult entertainment. A pool which was elliptical with stone steps submerged in the center was bordered by flat stone terrace elements of mica. A detached spa, was near the master bedroom and somewhat hidden from view by plantings. An overhead Arbor followed the terrace design curved to the end of the pool. The arbor was designed to provide shade in patterns, and created an easy design flow following the curved step-up to a raised section of the family entertainment patio area. The same terraced stonework, but raised 4" and grouted with blue color to help identify the elevation, enumerated the space for different activities and combined the architectural sense of it to that of the white-washed Arbor with the residence. The Arbor was placed at a high altitude so as not to interfere with the residential architecture, thus keeping the balance and extending its horizontal influence."

The most important feature in this scene is the pool and its coloring. From any position, this pool shows its character from the late shadows of the background and t he darker area caused by the depth, a factor in designing pools.

A small mound captured the architecture and balanced the addition.

Old railroad-tie steps
with brick paving between,
help create easy steps of 4"
and treads of 20".
On the near right is a
Sentinel Columnar White
Pine (Pinus strobus
v.fastigiata).
A Rhododendron Clatawbiense
(red) is good balance for the
Pine and lower ground cover.

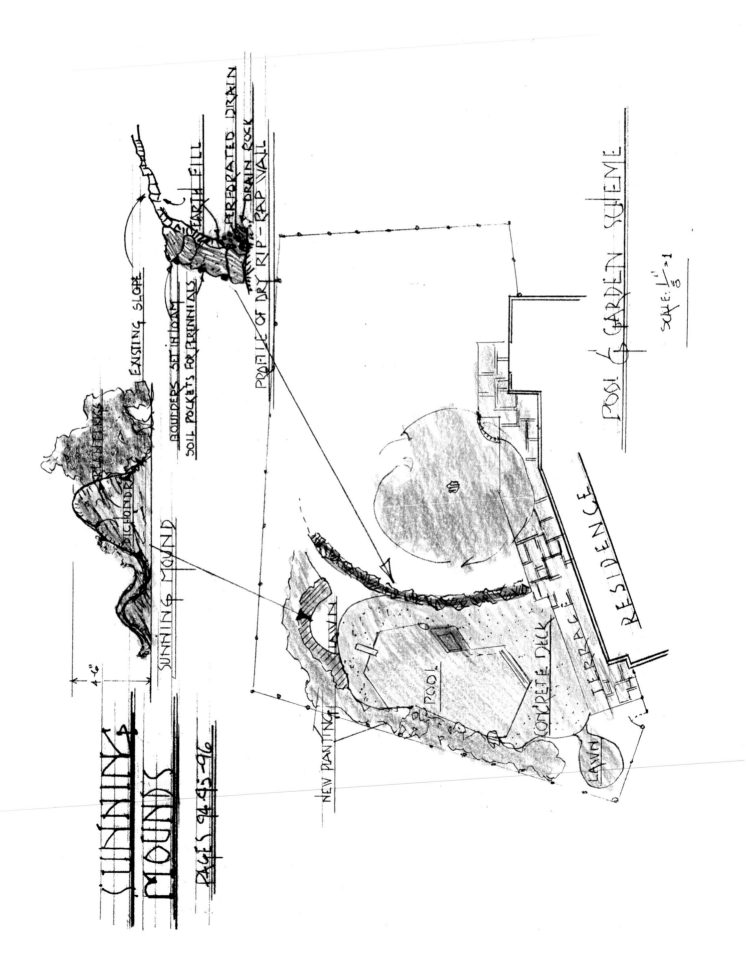

SUNNING & MOUNDS

PAGES 94·95·96

EXISTING SLOPE

BOULDERS SET IN LOAM
SOIL POCKETS FOR PERENNIALS

EARTH FILL

PERFORATED DRAIN

DRAIN ROCK

PROFILE OF DRY RIP-RAP WALL

PLANTING

BIG BOULDERS

SUNNING MOUND

4'·6'

NEW PLANTING

LAWN

POOL

CONCRETE DECK

TERRACE

RESIDENCE

LAWN

POOL & GARDEN SCHEME

SCALE: 1" = 5'

Sunning mounds are fun for kids as well as adults at poolside.
These are hand-formed with soil and covered with Dichondra, a
low ground hugging plant which spreads by root surface runners
and takes the summer heat and some shade.

Follow the Yellow Brick Road

Nothing exceeds using natural materials in a natural environment. The only exception to this maxim is concrete, which has many permutations for natural effects when used with inventiveness. There is much variety in the current inventory of materials, such as stamped designs in concrete, concrete pavers and flagstone patterns of all kinds. Some of the pavers used for driveways, patios and walks are tumbled so as to give the object a used look but, since they are all very much the same (except in some color variations), the laid surfaces inevitably look stiff and artificial.

Clay products like brick and its variations, on the other hand, are always changing with time and the surfaces develop a patina of historical significance. I don't use the artificial materials unless it is absolutely necessary for the sake of cost. Even then, one can rearrange the pattern by size or by using variants of natural materials to achieve a harmonious result.

Brick laid on a very firm fine gravel type of material called fines or stone dust gives the ultimate in a superior surface. It has a timeless look and a quality of strength, which exceeds all other materials available for this purpose. Many cities and villages in the Midwest and Eastern areas of this country still have the old brick roads and sidewalks, which remain quite usable, even after some 200 years. If these were made of concrete, they would have been replaced many times. These old brick streets evoke a certain permanence and fondness for the historical touch. Here antiquity shows, not only elegance but also superior endurance.

There is nothing more attractive than a brick walkway or patio, unless it is one that combines brick with some other material. A curve or bend adds an additional design twist.

Before the design is started on the site, it is imperative that the planned outline of the walk, terrace or patio is laid out on the ground before its shape is accepted. What is drawn on a plan is only the idea but, when you see it in full scale on the ground along with its comparison

A dry stonewall on a slant surrounds a wood plank deck patio with an intersecting brick entrance walk laid through the concrete driveway.

to other structural features, you may see that it needs to be altered for final artistic content. A garden hose is the perfect tool to outline.

When working with brick, first go to the yards with the client to view the types, colors and hardness. Often it is important to mix the types of brick, stones or flagstone to bring the color palette into synchronization with the surrounding natural characteristics of the site.

What are "soldiers" and "sailors?" These are bricks used for edging alongside a walk. Use this trick to differentiate them. When the fleet comes into port and all the sailors are aligned in a row from stem to stem, that's "sailors". When a platoon of soldiers marches past your front door, that's "soldiers". So, if you want your walkway to look a bit longer and narrower, line up your sailors. But, when a little more finish is desired or visual repetition to give the walk or border a thicker image, call out the soldiers.

Sometimes these types of borders can be used in a tactile manner. A sightless person can keep touching the borders with a foot to know the direction of a pathway and then change to the other pattern when approaching a crosswalk or turn. This technique alerts the individual to pay attention. Even if he or she knows where they are headed, there is an additional subliminal message directly underfoot. 🌀

The inside courtyard was designed to reduce the openness in this large area. The patterned brick is a mottled design of two different types. The outside of the squared Moroccan brick called 'cushwa' takes on a rougher texture but is a little smaller in dimension and size. This represents more of a European effect.

A delicate fencing and entrance wall leads to a shopping area, reflecting the quality of that being sold inside the store.

A speciman European Linden (Tilia Europa var. Redmond) stands regally besides the store

An attractive retail store entrance indicates historical antique articles for the buyer.

Detail of the circular brick pattern welcomes customers to the entrance of the store.

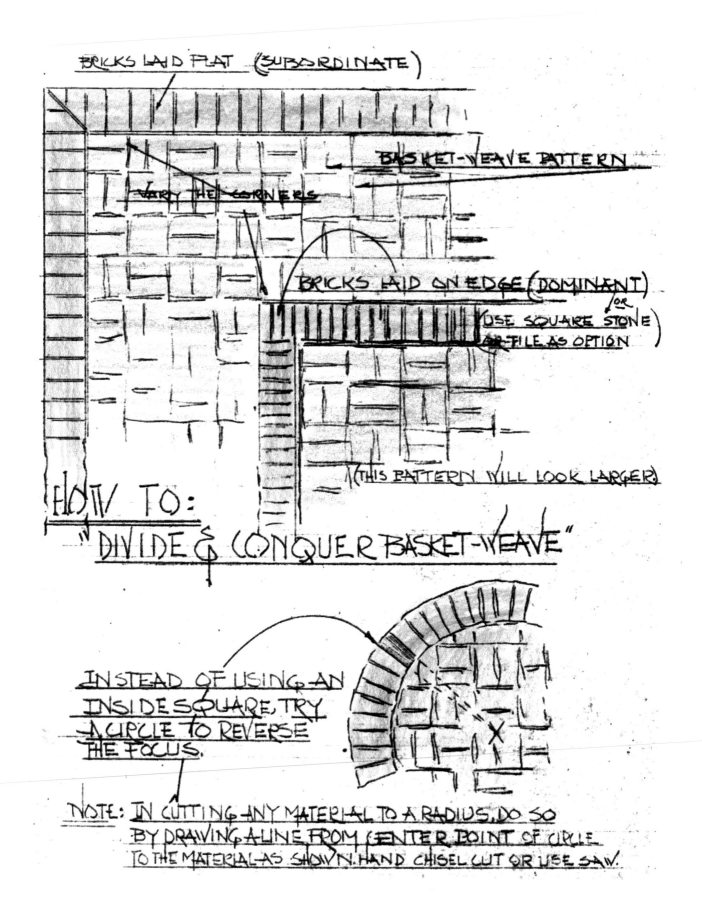

BRICKS LAID FLAT (SUBORDINATE)

VARY THE CORNERS

BASKET-WEAVE PATTERN

BRICKS LAID ON EDGE (DOMINANT)

(or USE SQUARE STONE OR TILE AS OPTION)

(THIS PATTERN WILL LOOK LARGER)

HOW TO:
"DIVIDE & CONQUER BASKET-WEAVE"

INSTEAD OF USING AN INSIDE SQUARE, TRY A CIRCLE TO REVERSE THE FOCUS.

NOTE: IN CUTTING ANY MATERIAL TO A RADIUS, DO SO BY DRAWING A LINE FROM CENTER POINT OF CIRCLE TO THE MATERIAL AS SHOWN. HAND CHISEL CUT OR USE SAW.

102

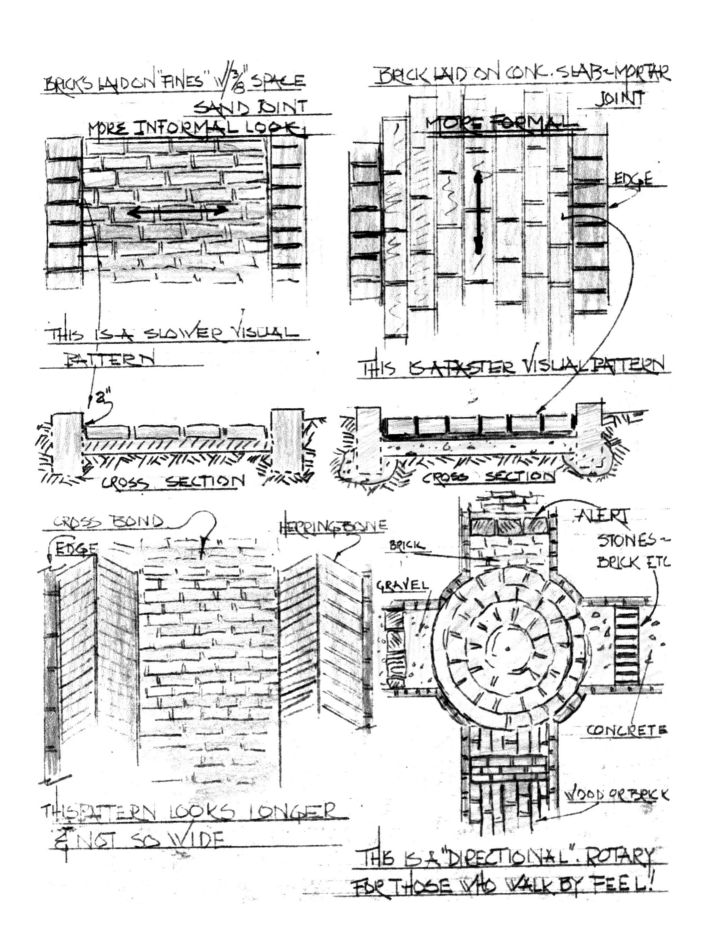

BRICKS LAID ON "FINES" W/3/8" SPACE
SAND JOINT
MORE INFORMAL LOOK.

THIS IS A SLOWER VISUAL
PATTERN

2"

CROSS SECTION

BRICK LAID ON CONC. SLAB~MORTAR
JOINT

MORE FORMAL

EDGE

THIS IS A FASTER VISUAL PATTERN

CROSS SECTION

CROSS BOND
EDGE

HERRINGBONE

THIS PATTERN LOOKS LONGER
& NOT SO WIDE

BRICK

GRAVEL

ALERT
STONES~
BRICK ETC

CONCRETE

WOOD OR BRICK

THIS IS A "DIRECTIONAL" ROTARY
FOR THOSE WHO WALK BY FEEL!

103

The Moroccan style gate provide an easy see through to the outer court yard as well as providing privacy. The steps in the background are arranged on a radius which pattern the entrance foyer. These steps are cantilevered 2" to provide a deep shadow against the 6" risers, which in turn develop the sculpture of the entrance bell tower architecture.

This colonial use of a brick pattern actually extends its surface area out beyond the patio structure, visually expanding its size and use.

The bricks in the innermost area of the circle are designed to form intercepting arcs. The bricks are cut in half and set "upwards". The grouting is wiped a little deeper to designate the brick edges and thus the repeating design.

Have your guest park in elegance as you meet them (Plan on pages 135 and 136).

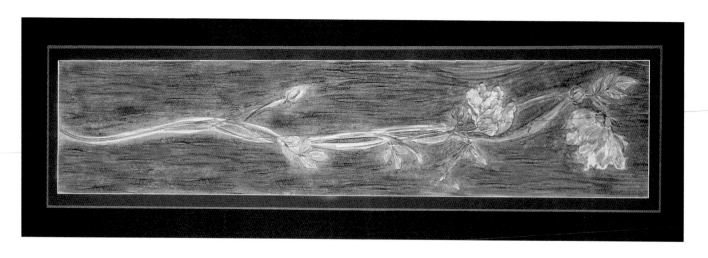

An intaglio design for an extended front entrance walk.

This garrison colonial backyard is owned by a man who is in the shoe business. The end hanging post has an antique "heal cutter" suspended by a chain. The cutter has a built-in iron bell ringer to call the kids. A brick "ripple" pattern emanates from the circular wall end.

This old sidewalk brick was taken from Boston's Beacon Hill in the early nineteen fifties. It has a marvelous warm patination from many years of pedestrian traffic. New bricks are now being made to emulate these oldies. The center of the 'round' shows a grindstone which originally came across the Atlantic as a ballast for the ships from England, all were 7' in diameter and dated 1696. When 'ground' down to 3', they were removed from the working spindle and rolled over an embankment into a river, thus found. The other side is dated early 1700s.

    At the far end of the walk is a granite slab for a step-up into the house. This piece was from the foundation of the Old Howard Burlesque Theatre located in Scollay Square in Boston taken during the reconstruction.

With a Lilac this size, the only design here is to wrap a terrace around it and enjoy the open lawn and a great run into the pool.

Guests enter the walkway by stepping up to the dark brick bordered circle. The walkway to the house was slightly curved inward to give more balance to the right side of the house and to visually lengthen the depth from the street.

109

"THE DESIGN WAS TO BE KEPT TO THE BACK YARD ONLY. They were in the process of deciding to add on a large wing to the house for solely entertainment purposes and to feature some exotic spa with a view east to the San Francisco Airport. Final plans excluded this wing and the garden developed as a low perimeter stonewall surrounding the yard in a rectangle with the inside area "poolet" or large spa, enhanced only by lawn area. Entrance to this area came from three directions: the most used would be from their master bedroom, (as shown above), and the other two more utilitarian in nature. The major piece of construction was the brick mosaic patio, done by David Chadwick, a master of brick mosaic. The dry stone wall, depicts English style sophistication with its arrangement of perennial colors in back of it. The wall ends curl down into the ground causing no disruption in movement and offer a type of introduction to the distant view. A tall Arborvitae hedge separates the end of the rear portion."

This shows the designer and craft in perfect unison, complex, yet pure.

110

A wooden gate greets
visitors as they enter an
herb and flower garden
court. The picture shows
its wooden hinges and
joinery, pegged and glued.

These steps begin at the pool
and curve up to a terraced area.

This adult sandpit for two saves time and driving to the beach. Plunge a few of your inside plants into the sand during the summer for effect as well as helping the plant vigor. During the winter the look changes to snow sculptures and deck sunning.

113

A study of Azaleas graces the front driveway entrance with a Redbud (Cercis canadensis) for the background.

Come to the Rescue with Bent and Fescue

Lawns are attractive and expensive, but not always environmentally correct. They certainly soak up water faster than a hundred buffalo wading in a river. The fertilizers and chemicals that have been discovered by the wizards to keep them looking nice unfortunately add to the environmental burden. Gasoline-powered lawn mowers don't help either, although they are nothing compared to our airplanes and cars. You might solve some of your own lawn problems ecologically by renting some goats or cattle, but what would your neighbors say?

This brings us to the huge industry of grass mixtures and sod. While the latter has the advantage of providing instant and cushy rolling green expanses, I must say that the best lawn is one that has been seeded. Of course, it takes some waiting for the result, but it's worth it. Like watching a baby grow from a toddler to a teen, it takes patience.

The sods available in today's market are undeniably good. They are soon ready for the mower. Within two weeks you can get out there and play football, have a party or go singin' in the rain in your bare feet. It's like buying an oriental or even a hardwood floor. The convenience is hard to beat.

Seeding, on the other hand, gives you one huge advantage in the eventual composition of the turf. It always ensures the best lawn because you can choose your own type of seed. Costwise, the installation is about the same, since most soils require a three or four inch layer of coarse sand mixed in to the top of the prepared surface. This allows better drainage so that the grass roots can sink deeper into the soil.

115

*If your sideyard looks too straight or crowded, take it apart and put in a slight curve with a boundary for some
small gravel for walking (See page 119). Bring out your houseplants and orchids, giving them a vacation for the summer.*

❶

One of the best overall seed mixtures is a combination of Penn Lawn Fescue, Bent and Kentucky Blue. There are two varieties of Fescue. One is a wide-bladed grass and is the most popular, due to its rough and hardy texture mostly used on athletic fields. The other variety, the one that I maintain is the best for its fine slim needle-like leaf, is the Penn Lawn or Creeping Red Fescue. This variety likes sun and shade alike and it sends its roots deeper than most. With the addition of a small amount of Bent which is the grass used on putting greens, the softness factor is added. Finally, the Kentucky Blue grass, which has a wider leaf blade, adds a lustrous component, making the lawn look elegant and graceful. It is my opinion that this mixture of grasses is as lovely and rich as you can get. It takes longer for it to grow (one of the major reasons it isn't popular with the producers of sod grasses) but, if you have the patience and want the best, this is the preferred method.

The very best time to seed a lawn is from November to March, giving the seed a chance to set into the soil bed during the winter months. When the warm spells begin, it will then germinate and grow long before the weedy competition elbows in.

To prepare the soil for seeding, one should fully remove already-existing weeds by first applying a soil-sterilizing chemical such as Roundup and let it set for at least 45 days. Then, after seeding, water the area once or twice a week. By the time May arrives, the grasses should be germinated and starting to thicken. One way to hasten the growth at this point is to apply an organic fertilizer once a week. Keep it watered only on the top, not deeply, three or four times a day for no more than three or four minutes. Then, as the grass matures, change the fertilizer to a more concentrated mix of nitrogen, phosphorus and potassium, in a mixture of an organic 20-10-10, combined with a weed killer. This

"The Source" by Fredrick Hart

should take care of whatever the mower can't discourage. All this maintenance will require approximately one full spring, summer and fall. After that you should have the most durable and beautiful lawn around. Use a reel mower if possible.

A final word about the other broadleaf fescue sods, now the most popular turf type on the market. There are many varieties and mixtures of grasses such as Common Rye, Kentucky Blue and Colonial Bent. Since developing a lawn with the needle-type fescue (Penn Lawn Fescue) takes longer, these other grasses are the alternative for instant gratification. If you need to have the lawn party next week, this is the way to go.

Otherwise, the lengthier process described earlier is well worth the wait. A good seed mix might be as follows:

50% Pen Lawn Creeping Red Fescue

35% Kentucky Blue

10% Bent

5% Annual Rye

If your sideyard looks too straight or crowded, take it apart and put in a slight curve with a boundary for some small gravel for walking (See page 119). Bring out your houseplants and orchids, giving them a vacation for the summer.

118

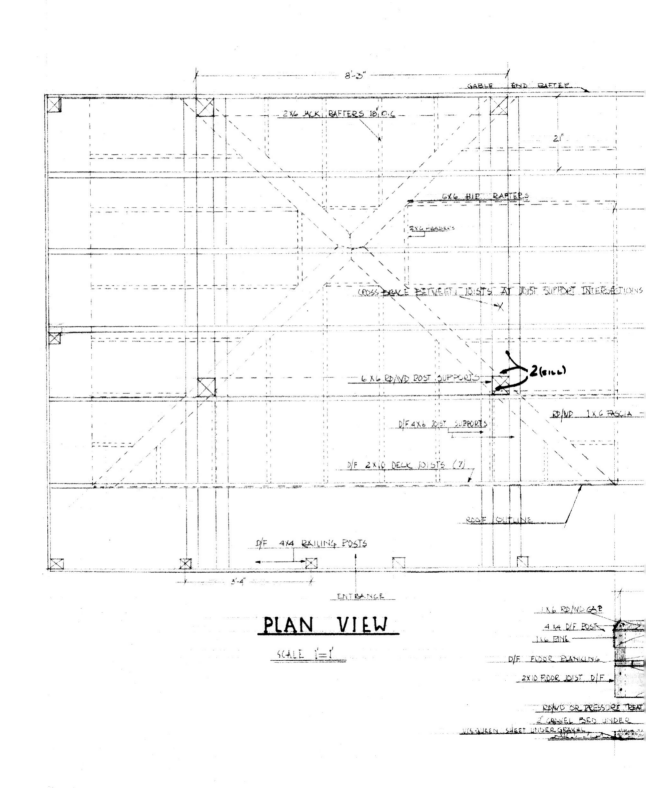

8'-3"

GABLE END RAFTER

2X6 JACK RAFTERS 18" O.C.

21"

6X6 HIP RAFTERS

2X6 HEADERS

CROSS BRACE BETWEEN JOISTS AT JOIST SUPPORT INTERSECTIONS

2(SILL)

6 X 6 RD/WD POST SUPPORTS

RD/WD 1X6 FASCIA

D/F 4X6 JOIST SUPPORTS

D/F 2X10 DECK JOISTS (7)

ROOF OUTLINE

D/F 4X4 RAILING POSTS

3'-4"

ENTRANCE

PLAN VIEW

SCALE 1"=1'

1X6 RD/WD GAP

4 X4 D/F POST

1X6 PINE

D/F FLOOR PLANKING

2X10 FLOOR JOIST D/F

RD/WD OR PRESSURE TREAT

2" GRAVEL BED UNDER

VISQUEEN SHEET UNDER GRAVEL

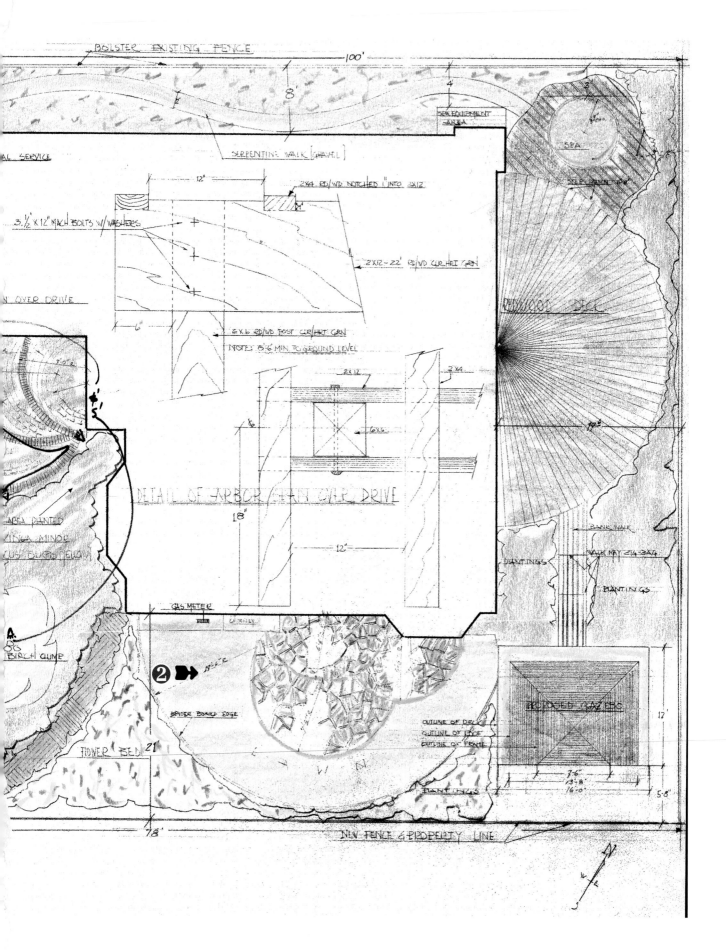

BOLSTER EXISTING FENCE

100'

8'

4'

SPA EQUIPMENT
AREA

SPA

SEE DTL ON DWG

AL SERVICE

SERPENTINE WALK [GRAVEL]

12"

2X4 RD/WD NOTCHED 1" INTO 2X12

3.½" X 12" MACH BOLTS W/ WASHERS

2X12 - 22' RD/WD CLR/HRT GRN

N' OVER DRIVE

6"

6 X 6 RD/WD POST CLR/HRT GRN

NOTE: 8'-6" MIN TO GROUND LEVEL

REDWOOD DECK

AREA PLANTED
VINCA MINOR

BANE WALK

PLANTINGS

WALK MAY 2'6-3X4

PLANTINGS

DETAIL OF ARBOR START OVER DRIVE

2X12

2X4

6X6

6"

18"

12"

A

BIRCH CLUMP

GAS METER

CHIMNEY

② ➡

BENDER BOARD EDGE

OUTLINE OF DEC
OUTLINE OF EDGE
OUTLINE OF FRAME

PROPOSED GAZEBO

12'

FLOWER BED 21'

3'-6"
13'-8"
16'-0"

5'-8"

18'

NEW FENCE & PROPERTY LINE

N

W   E

S

120

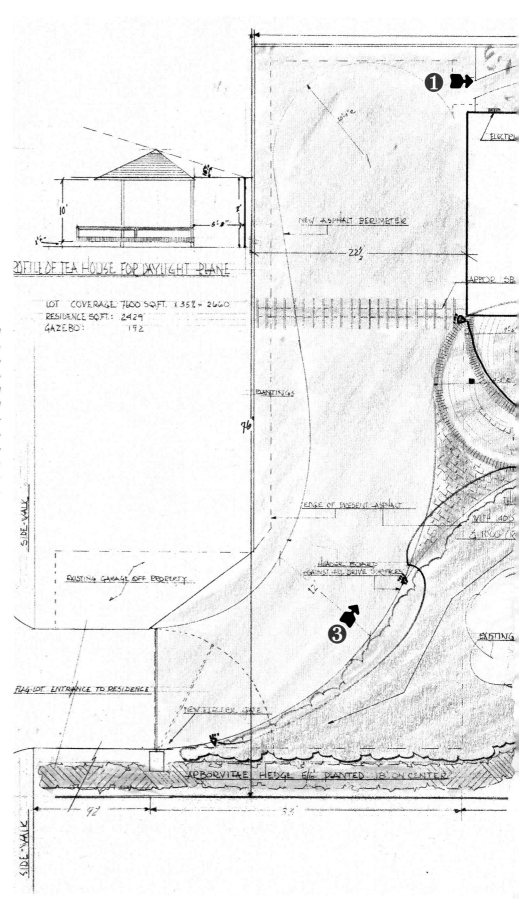

PROFILE OF TEA HOUSE FOR DAYLIGHT PLANE

LOT COVERAGE 7600 SQ.FT. X 35% = 2660
RESIDENCE SQ.FT.: 2429
GAZEBO: 192

A flag-lot property offers an "extended axis" entrance. The Arborvitae hedging (south east side) guides and nicely introduces one to the front entrance area. The left side (NNW) is a small curved pathway of Orchids and small perenials nad which leads to the rear Spa and large redwood deck. Opposite the deck is a Tea House made joinery style. The interior and very spacious living room leads out to a stone-moss terrace bounded by lawn and perenials

NEW ASPHALT PERIMETER

PLANTINGS

EDGE OF PRESENT ASPHALT

HEADER BOARD AGAINST HIL DRIVE SURFACE

EXISTING GARAGE OFF PROPERTY

FLAG-LOT ENTRANCE TO RESIDENCE

SIDE-WALK

ARBORVITAE HEDGE 6/6 PLANTED 18' ON CENTER

119

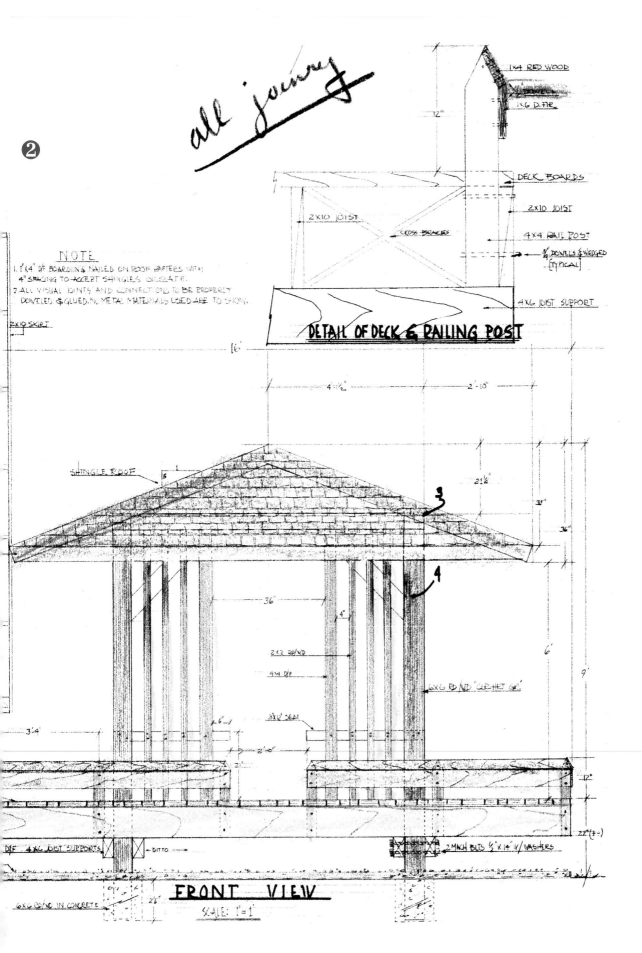

❷

all journey

1X4 RED WOOD

1X6 D. FIR

12"

DECK BOARDS

2X10 JOIST

CROSS BRACES

4X4 RAIL POST

2X10 JOIST

¾ DOWELS & WEDGED [TYPICAL]

4X6 JOIST SUPPORT

DETAIL OF DECK & RAILING POST

NOTE
1. 1"X4" D/F BOARDING NAILED ON ROOF RAFTERS WITH
   4" SPACING TO ACCEPT SHINGLES OR SLATE.
2. ALL VISUAL JOINTS AND CONNECTIONS TO BE PROPERLY
   DOWELED & GLUED. NO METAL MATERIALS USED ARE TO SHOW.

2X10 SKIRT

16'

4'-1½"   2'-10"

2'1½"

31"

36"

SHINGLE ROOF

5

3

4

6'

9'

36"

4"

2X2 RD/WD

4X4 D/F

6X6 RD/WD "CLR HT GR"

6"

3'X8" SEAT

2'-0"

3'4

2'

12"

22"(+-)

D/F 4X6 JOIST SUPPORTS   DITTO   2 MACH BLTS ½" X 14" W/ WASHERS

6X6 RD/WD IN CONCRETE   2'   2'

FRONT VIEW
SCALE: 1"=1'

122

❸

❷

"THE ENTRANCE WAS QUITE NONDESCRIPT SO THE IMPACT AREA WAS THE APPROACH AND OPENING TO THE FRONT ENTRANCE. Here we rearranged the front vestibule, from an ordinary two-step to the driveway and swept it around a part of the house front giving the entrance a different direction of approach. A tall evergreen hedge separated the right sideyard and behind it was another small rock garden terrace which came from the dining room. This little sitting area was made up of Arizona moss rock set on topsoil. The voids between the stones were chinked with Veronica repens, a small leafed evergreen creeper which has tolerance for traffic and exposure.

At the far corner of the lot, and before one turns to the backyard, was a Tea House. The structure was made up entirely of joinery. Many of these fittings were part of the visual pleasure. Upon sitting on one of the thick pine benches, one could look across the backyard to the semicircular wood decking. Access to this deck was by stepping on and over several large 36" Cypress log ends which were at uneven heights and placed at stepping widths. These stumps were surrounded by a sea of Pachysandra, an evergreen ground cover. The deck was made of 2"x12" redwood cut from one end diagonally, to the opposite end, therefore resulting in a piece of wood that was 12" wide at one end and pointed at the other. These pieces were then placed with the pointed ends at the radial position.

At the far end of the lot and touching this deck was a spa, set into the ground a bit lower than the deck. Surrounding the spa, for deck covering, were hundreds of 4"x4"x4" pieces of wood all tightly fitted to each other. This kept consistency of materials needed for such a tight space and yet offed a relief to the pattern which dominated the deck proper. Finally, going down the other side of the property, we removed a concrete utility walk and replaced this with a serpentine one of 30" wide filled with grey fines (a fine compacting sand and gravel mix). Along this meandering way the owners opted to plant their orchids and choice perennials."

123

*There are times when a garden wall needs that extra 'fling.' Try something such as this Horsetail (Equisetum).
Most likely you will enjoy the coloration of the wall stones (pinks) and all the different shadows as well.*

*Moving from one garden area to the next requires a pause before proceeding.
Here, some large plant urns flank an iron gate which is enough to hold one's tempo and thought prior to entering.*

A raised spa (18") covered with small mosaic pieces
set a prescribed pattern of movement and colors.

A nighttime scene of a spa, pool, and raised pool wall. Above the wall, the iron work depicts a celestial motif using Byzantine glass mosaics. This scene amplifies skyward movements of shooting stars with distant planets and galaxies in the background, represented by the Rhododendrons in colors of pink, white, red, and yellow. On the raised bondbeam of the pool, a cityscape is seen silhouetted against a clear nighttime sky of stars and other celestial bodies. To the left, on the spa is a fountain made of the same Byzantine mosaic. Its interpretation is one of center Earth's more fiery and active movement amplified by the motion of the water flowing down and through the raised glass elements.

Darwin tulip

Pooling Resources

A number of years ago I was asked to be a judge in a regional pool competition. I accepted gladly and soon was sent all kinds of pictures of pools done by different contractors. I looked at them, studied them and, in time, sent them back. The head of the project called me and said: "Thanks, but you didn't give anybody first prize."

"That's right," I replied. "Nobody deserved first prize!"

He was dumfounded; being of the mind that a prize had to be awarded. But, if not merited by the correct elements of art, setting and level of construction work, how can a prize be given?

Choosing the color of the plaster is a crucial decision as this is where the color of water takes its inference. Water is always clear; its color comes from the reflective material under or around it. The choices are many: black, gray-black, blues, blue-green, and green. Each has its own character of reflection or show of depth and must be considered in planning. Do you wish to catch the canopy of tree

The pool-edge action is the main feature and its deck, made of washed stone aggregate, cantilevers over the edge of the pool by two inches, leaving a darker shadow line under the entire curvature. This effect gives a little more drama to the pool color of a Caribbean green, or granny apple. One portion of the decking on the left is raised by four inches to accomodate a large sitting area.

and sky silhouette, create a feeling of depth or provides an invigorating apple green color, as if straight from the Caribbean?

Just as there are a myriad color choices, pools today come in any and every shape and style under the sun. Nevertheless, water enclosures can be considered an intimate extension of our fantasies and designing them for smaller spaces calls for much sensitivity in the use of soft plantings and groundcover surrounds, as well as carefully-placed landscape lighting.

Also available and highly desirable when planning a residential pool, is the use of a spa. In addition to a therapeutic value, the spa often has a built-in waterfall which is a nice visual extension to one's yard. Listening to the quiet sound of its spill can be comforting.

While waterfalls and fountains can greatly extend the pleasures of sight and sound, they must be carefully adjusted for volume.

Once, when setting a fountain in a small villa walled garden, the owner requested that I keep the water spouting as high as possible, in order to overcome some outside traffic noise. As we worked on the project in other areas of the garden, I gradually decreased the fountain in height so that,

A view from the top! A double staircase (pg.180) leads down to this area of the pool. In order to lessen the large concrete deck area, a 'strip' deck was designed to create a warmer touch and relate to the wooded background.

within a few weeks, it was down to a quiet purr. Not a word was said, as the client having gradually adjusted to listening to the sound of the fountain and not the traffic.

The same principle applies to all water art forms. Beauty can be, not only in the eye, but in the ear of the beholder. 🪷

This round pool has a three foot depth at the edges and goes to nine feet. With a white plaster under coat, the pool colors are much darker in the center and lighter around the circumference, thus making the pool look larger than it is (20'). During the construction of the pool decking area, of chocolate color flagstone, several pockets were made available for plantings. To the left is a stone diving rock .

The waterfall was added after the pool was built and some of the raised brick pool wall had to be cut for the stone spillway with the water being pumped from the pool. Note the 'tilted arbor' in front of the fence property line. This was built to serve as a high screen barrier with vines.

"*THE LEAD CAME FROM A SALES FRIEND. The pool was already established and I was to landscape the back yard area. They wanted a dressing room, a waterfall, and an arbor. They specifically requested privacy from their back yard neighbor whose 'dough-boy' pool was decked high enough for the neighbors to easily peer over the fence and watch the action. I suggested a 'tilted' Arbor for this and planted with grape vines. The waterfall was not difficult but, as I see it now, one of the best thought out designs I have done yet for this purpose. In making this object, I fell into the pool several times attempting to cement rocks to the ledge of the raised bond beam wall. Since I was using lamp black to color the mortar one can imagine the sight of the pool water when I got finished. The bathhouse was another matter. One would have to enter it to see the intricate lap work for strength. It is round with a romanesque peak. The bath house is wrapped with bender board. The children thought it was a great place to play.*"

A backyard pool and spa with a boulder diving rock is enhanced with a friendly clump of S antolina chamaecparissus (below). Japanese flavor type fencing favors views of adjacent golf course (above).

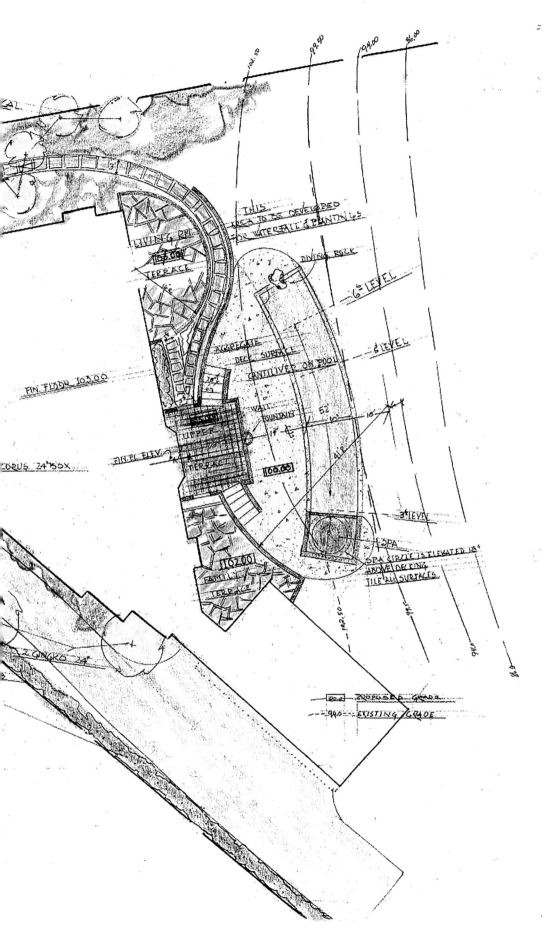

136

406

405

404

PLANTINGS

CONTRACT LIMIT LINE

402

WALL

STEPS

402.25

TERRACE 401.25

SALTED BROWN CONCRETE

400

FIN. FLR 401.

398

396

DRIVEWAY

CONTRACT LIMIT LINE

8' SCREEN

DAYLIGHT DRAINS

N

133

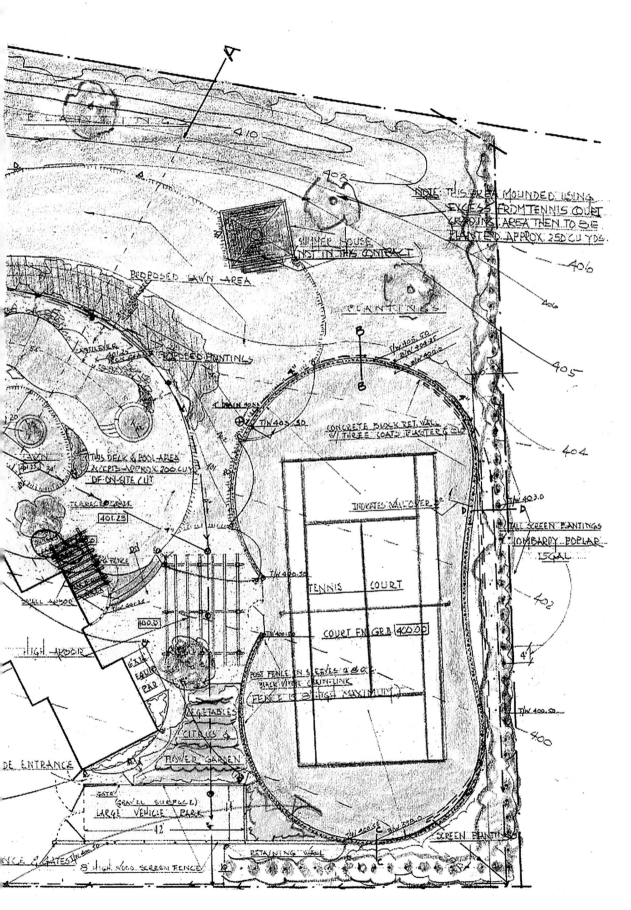

PLEASE LIFT →

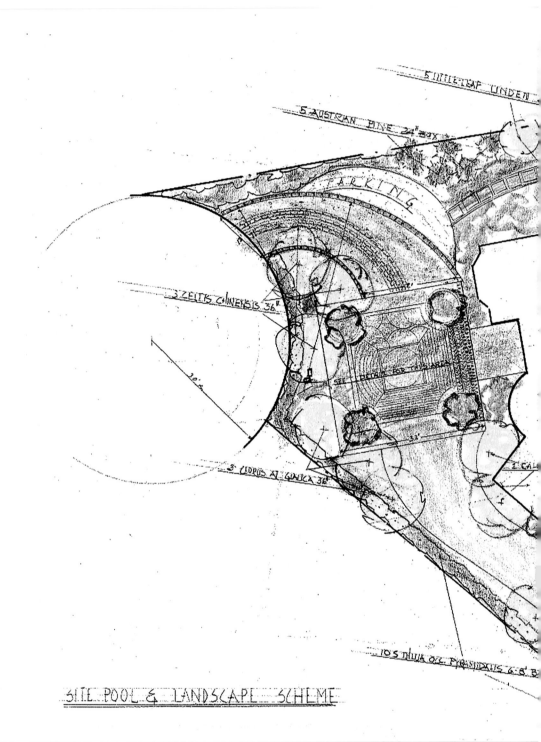

5 LITTLELEAF LINDEN

5 AUSTRIAN PINE 2'-3'X

PARKING

3 ZELTIS CHINENSIS 36"

SEE DETAIL FOR 1" GARDEN

3 CEDRUS AT GLAUCA 36

2' GAL

10 S THUJA OCC PYRAMIDALIS 6-8' B

SITE POOL & LANDSCAPE SCHEME

AMES M. CHADWICK ASSOCIATES — 101 CHURCH ST #6 LOS GATOS CA   11-2-8

SCALE ⅛'-1'

N

The scene shows the stairway access up to this partially sunken spa. Rimmed by some smooth waterwash stones. Irish moss is planted en mass for relaxing while puddling one's toes.

137

Tranquil.

"THIS IS A LAP POOL CONCEPT. Best shots are those reciprocal ones allowing for reflections to enhance. A perennial garden access is by means of a steel foot bridge which is planted with moss. The bridge was thus designed with 'delicate' in mind so as not to overtake the scene. On the other side of the pool which is used for normal passage, redwood logs, (the still bark on), are placed upon the soil, log to log. Moss was then chinked between the voids creating a natural look, soft on the feet. Near the house end of pool, a spa is situated and it is surrounded by redwood decking". (See page 131)

A lap pool also serves as a place to meditate. The pool narrows where a steel bridge provides an access to the perennial beds opposite. The moss-covered bridge is irrigated from each side. The inside pool walls were plastered green/black which accounts for its high reflective value.

This circumference is free-form in shape, thus designing a deck for it should be the same, only different. Here the deck boards follow a visual design "as you go". The grain coloration gives the design an "upbeat" flavor.

139

A CANTILEVER EDGE TO POOL

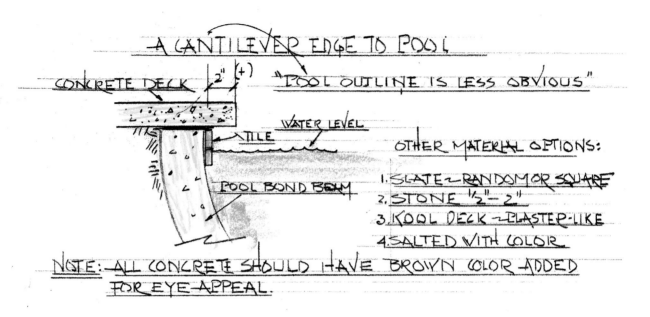

CONCRETE DECK   2" (+)   "POOL OUTLINE IS LESS OBVIOUS"

WATER LEVEL

TILE

POOL BOND BEAM

OTHER MATERIAL OPTIONS:
1. SLATE~RANDOM OR SQUARE
2. STONE "½"-2"
3. KOOL DECK~PLASTER-LIKE
4. SALTED WITH COLOR

NOTE: ALL CONCRETE SHOULD HAVE BROWN COLOR ADDED FOR EYE-APPEAL.

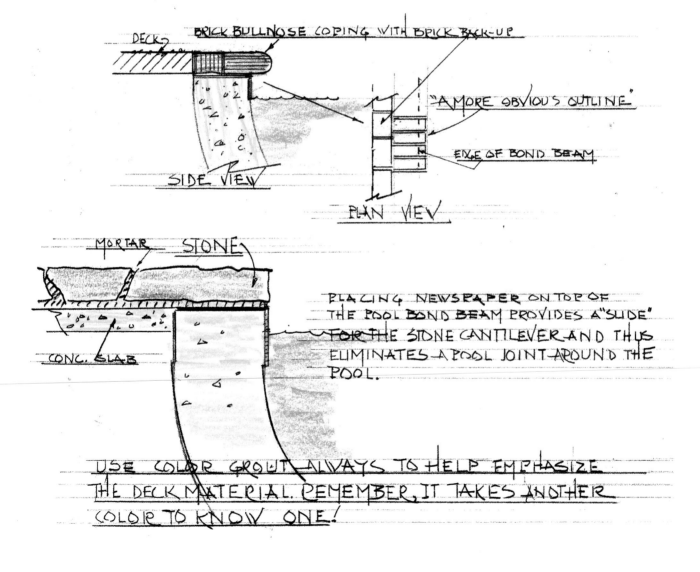

DECK   BRICK BULLNOSE COPING WITH BRICK BACK-UP

"A MORE OBVIOUS OUTLINE"

EDGE OF BOND BEAM

SIDE VIEW

PLAN VIEW

MORTAR   STONE

CONC. SLAB

PLACING NEWSPAPER ON TOP OF THE POOL BOND BEAM PROVIDES A "SLIDE" FOR THE STONE CANTILEVER AND THUS ELIMINATES A POOL JOINT AROUND THE POOL.

USE COLOR GROUT ALWAYS TO HELP EMPHASIZE THE DECK MATERIAL. REMEMBER, IT TAKES ANOTHER COLOR TO KNOW ONE!

ANOTHER POOL IDEA!

(THE WATER RIDES OVER THE TILE SURFACE)

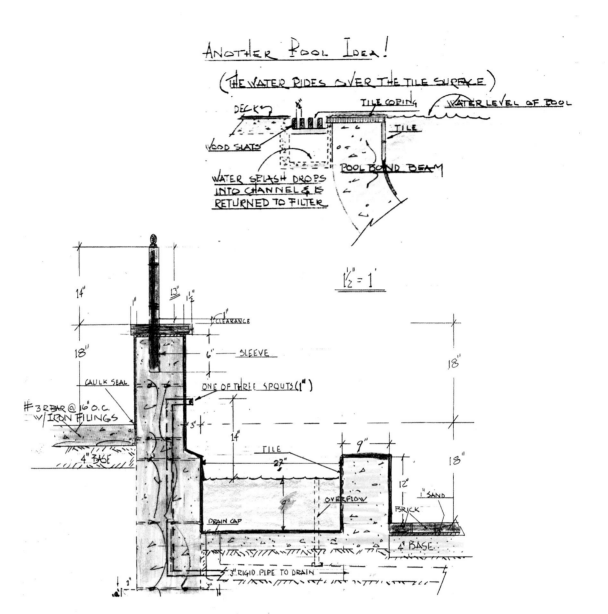

DECK

TILE COPING   WATER LEVEL OF POOL

WOOD SLATS   TILE

WATER SPLASH DROPS
INTO CHANNEL & IS
RETURNED TO FILTER   POOL BOND BEAM

$1\frac{1}{2}" = 1'$

14"
18"
1"
13" 1½"
1" CLEARANCE
6"   SLEEVE
CAULK SEAL
ONE OF THREE SPOUTS (1")
#3 REBAR @ 16" O.C.
W/ IRON FILINGS
3"
4" BASE
14"
TILE
27"
OVERFLOW
9"
DRAIN CAP
18"
18"
9"
12"
1" SAND
BRICK
4" BASE
3" RIGID PIPE TO DRAIN
3"
3"

SOME DRIVE SURFACE IDEAS

PLANT GRASS OR VERONICA REPEN
BETWEEN STONES

1. 4"-6" THICK STONES SET FIRMLY INTO GROUND

2. A "COUNTRY" LOOK IS PENETRATION-TYPE

THIS DRIVE SURFACE IS LOW KEY & COLORFULL.
IT IS MADE BY LAYING DOWN 2-4" OF 1½" CRUSHED
STONE - ROLLED & THEN THE ROCK IS COATED
WITH AN ASPHALT EMULSION & LET SET FOR A
DAY OR TWO. THEN ANOTHER COAT OF ASPHALT
EMULSION IS APPLIED & AT ONCE SMALLER
CRUSHED ROCK (ANY COLOR) IS THROWN OVER THIS AREA
& ROLLED INTO VOIDS. EXCESS STONE MAY BE REMOVED

141

*Driveways are too utilitarian in the front, but this one
has become an integral part of the entire design scheme.*

*Note the strong sweeping motion of the brick entrance which starts
its journey from the street and follows through to the house entrance.*

This formal design is made up of dwarf English boxwood hedging and English lavender centers creating an organized design function which is eye catching.

144

Enjoyment is created by strolling through this "slow" gate. The gate is supported on one side by a heavy iron rod. Its curling motion actually starts at the top of the woodpost and then transfers its motion from the gate itself to the iron crook push bar.

An entrance lamp glows against the moonlight.

A master of the garden is the Delphinium.

Thunbergia gregorii

White Dawn climbing rose.

146

A step alert pattern provides a visual for the walk.

What else . . . Bouganvillea peeking through the slats.

The garbage cans are camouflaged .

Utilities are enclosed.

148

A quiet setting of stone, water, and plants creates the spirit and soul of contemplation.

A tiny path to the hot tub is created for a soft footpath amongst ferns, Taro poi, Mosses, etc.
"The Drinker" by David Goode

The sunken barbeque area has a floor of woodblock (4"x4"x4") set on a concrete slab.

"Bark-on" redwood posts serve as a sitting wall.

151

A small terrace controlled by one Sophora japonica instills quietness.

Inside or out, the reflective combinations exist.

*The front portico surface consists of brick cut to
a fan design with a strong marble accent.*

*After pouring the concrete for this small side garden walk, the
flagstone was wiggled into the wet cement, smoothed and then
washed with a hose to expose the aggregate.*

The family is ready for the holiday.

Watch out for the guard dog on duty!

This iron gate exudes charm because of its curvature which also adds parking space on the public side and a private family space..

The stairway was built to gain outside extra access to a basement room. The intent is to create as much color as possible with minmum lighting. It is a drop of 10' and outside protecting walls have two built-in planters which are generously planted with foliage and color added in season. The floor, steps with ledges, are Vermont Flagstone with a higher percentage than usual (25%) of the red to highlight the views from inside the house. The entrance down is clearly identified by a semi-circle done in a Rollock style brick.

Turning the corner one hears the water trickling under the foliage with Taro poi and two Black Pine (Pinus thunbergi) ready to direct.

An inviting garden terrace with a "second look" has added reflections of beauty.

Remember that woodpile which sits in the back forty? Put it to use this way when making a quiet garden pathway and chink it here and there. Not only does it feel good, but it looks good. The earth's critters will love to soften it up for you!

158

A raised Vermont flagstone terrace and a
sunken spa overlook the pool and backyard.
The multi-colored stone affords a lively sense
of play which is offset by a background of
flowering shrubs.

Curved steps lead up to a deck on the main floor
of the house. Set amidst European White Birch,
the spiral stairs lend an attractive balance.

159

Bellis perennis

Wood You Like To

The famous author H. G. Wells dreamed up a Time Machine. I have my own personal mechanism for going back in time: several books in my library written by Eric Sloane, an illustrator and author of an earlier day. Sloane has penned some 20 volumes on the Early American and Colonial Periods. There are none better describing the beginnings of this country from the standpoint of how we lived and survived.

Detailed history of how the settlers of this country managed the workday and consulted one another on life, liberty and the pursuit of happiness is right there in those pages and should be required reading for all young students. It's probably too late for anyone after high school since life after that is wound up at warp speed. People have all they can do to keep up with the electronic age.

Sloane's concepts bring me back to the basics, enabling me to step into someone's life and

Upstairs, downstairs...note the "broken" stone wall
connection for obscurance (See page 41-42).

160

A main floor balcony was opened for this entrance sweep to the lower informal and formal gardens. The fabrication of the stair framework was done off-site and lowered into position with the help of a crane. The steps were figured on a six and 18 (6' risers & 18' treads) ratio. A more formal area was elevated 24". The lower patio was used for breakfasting and teas. The design of a downward radius of the stair gives a pleasant gliding perspective from the upper main living floor. In building the larger stone wall which connects to and is part of the formal garden frame, the left ninety degree turn is left undone, a design idea for it to blend more into the existing growth.

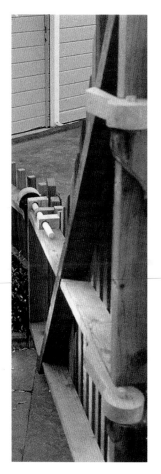

add some of those crafty elements of an earlier day into their landscape.

My youth was spent in a rural town in northern Maine where many of the old-timers were still plying their trades and lacing their homespun anecdotes with a heaping spoonful of vocabulary. Their way of speaking has stuck with me until today. Accordingly, when I say to a friend or a client: "that's what keeps the rabbit's tail short," I simply mean that sometimes things don't go as planned and maybe it's time to move on.

When something like that pops out, I have seen clients look at me with a smile that veers between amusement and questioning of my mental status, but eventually they come to realize it's only my way of adding a little lavender to the pot of life. It also is true that, when a boat is becalmed because of no wind, it may be time to sit down and contemplate the earthworms on land.

Believe it or not, all this has a practical application. By incorporating some of these inventive folk-proven ways of dealing with life into the current environment of busy people and machines, a welcome simplicity can be added. One way of adding simplicity is to design a wooden gate with wood hinges and wood slide closures that can be adjusted to close on their own, eliminating the need for any springs. Using dowels and glue on all the mortise and tenon joints, the gate is the last thing standing when the cows come home. No nuts or bolts, only what is grown in the woods. Such gates were made at a time when nothing else was available except what you could saw out

162

This was a delight to design and construct., using all Douglas Fir, mortised with hardwood pegs and glued.

163

A hilltop wood deck and pathway leads to a major lawn area.

of a tree trunk or salvage as scrap after putting up a door for the chicken house. It is exactly these memories of actual down-home carpentry that engage the client with their usefulness and inventiveness.

I once remember seeing a mailbox made with an old boot, nailed by the toe into a post alongside the road. The open part of the boot where the foot went faced the road and was where the mail was placed by the driver of the stage, the coach that went from town to town down dusty lanes to deliver mail and the occasional passenger.

It is necessary for a good designer, after going through the rigors of a formal education, to learn some of this history so that it can be demonstrated with art and humor. The old ways of doing things are rapidly being lost in the world of modern technology but they still are ripe fodder for contemporary residential landscape design. Colonial principles and traditional touches, when added to a finished piece of work, show that mastering a trade or profession is a personal gift, not only to the client, but also to oneself.

Designers should always be on the lookout for new or adaptable possibilities for decks, walks or any other landscape-related structures. For example, instead of doing the usual squares, rectangles

or sharp cornered designs that almost always are seen, one should look for design ideas that hang, such as wall coverings or drapes, or check out brick patterns and woodwork on older estate houses. You can even study a railway track for its curvature, which satisfies the instinct for depth and strength.

You might examine the inside of a canoe and note the interesting striations of widening cedar strips converging to an end. The motion is perfect and smooth with a sensual, yet practical, emotional effect. Once, when watching such a canoe being built, the idea came to me to flatten the plane of the structure and make a deck by using a slim board of 1"x2" lumber, standing on edge. The wood can be bent up to its stress point (easy to do after soaking it in a pool) and a curvature developed that enhances the surrounding landscape. The visual flow of proportions and density is very serene.

Another idea both practical and innovative is to use 4"x4"x4" blocks of wood for a

Hand made for the client, this pineapple greeting finial has offered many years of gentility and Godspeed

walkway or even a low profile decking (See page 166). I remember, back in Junior High School when taking manual training classes that all the flooring was made of this size block. Occasionally, some dolt would drop one of the hard-to-come-by chisels or a delicate tool. The wooden floor became a saving grace for the tool and its two-legged wielder. The wooden floor also was very comfortable to stand on for long class periods.

This kind of flooring, treated or made of redwood, pine or pressure-treated Douglas fir and laid on a firm concrete base, will last indefinitely. One

Obviously the are no nails, bolts or (code) advice. It's been there for ninety years, and it has charm.

A 1" x 2" strip deck follows the pool with flowing motion. This is very theraputic on the feet and very safe as well.

"THIS PROJECT CAME OUT QUITE WELL despite the many difficulties with the owner. The back yard required a lap pool (10'x40') but there was very little space to put this structure, plus a good sized decking attached to the house as well. One way to work this problem out was to pinch in the pool on one side and use this contour as the deck as well. We decided on using the Douglas Fir 1"x2" strips to visually extend the areas space and also to replicate the wavy motion of the water. The far side of the pool allowed only 2' of space. In this area we planted and constructed a small waterfall that faced the interior house views."

More modern than in its original 1940's inception, this indoor/outdoor effect goes right to the pool. The motion derived from placing 1"x2" fir strips visibly extends the distance is making it quite dramatic. This design requires on-the-job deliberations with the motion being develop as the wood is being assembled.

of the pleasures of such a finished product is the appearance of the flower-like pattern of the rings in the wood. Best of all, try walking on it with bare feet. It's absolutely therapeutic!

The goal here is to begin looking for ideas in someone else's backyard. Glance through high fashion women's magazines and subscribe to an upscale publication which illustrates country homes. The real estate section alone will provide enough ideas to last longer than your brain can contemplate. Many of these photographs show marvelous architectural work in wood and brick, reflecting extraordinary design and taste. Simplicity and elegance go hand in hand.

What can you do with all this? Suppose you see a wonderful wall on a building. Envision it flat on the ground and then design it for your particular site area. If an intricate mosaic garden outline or parterre is the problem, buy a book on Oriental rugs to find the solution.

The key to individuality is to put your foot in someone else's pond. Adapt. Find your ideas in other mediums and spend less time wandering the globe to visit famous gardens for ideas. Truly successful designers dig holes in the ground like everyone else, but they find a better way to think about it. So think about it. The only way to express diversity and spark intuition is to become totally involved. It

A Zen motif using douglas fir in motion is very quiet-like, serene and meditative.

isn't enough to draw plans and hand them over to someone else to interpret. You must follow through from the initial design to the hands-on completion of the craft. 🌀

"THIS PROJECT WAS UNUSUAL IN THAT IT WAS ONE OF THE VERY FEW I DESIGNED ONLY, BUT DID NOT CONSTRUCT. The client wished to do it himself. At the time he was traveling all around the world for his company. His time at home was preciously devoted to his family and home. What a family, with seven children, plus they always had a foreign student living with them as well. She was a very beautiful woman and very ambitious with her time. She involved herself with all kinds of small enterprises that developed the family regimen. Their needs were to give new life to their back yard. A pool surrounded by old concrete walks and a property fencing was it. It looked pretty tacky. The design came out to be a type of wood decking that flowed. In other words, the deck surface was accepted in order to build **over** the existing concrete, and wood was the best possibility realistically.

The next problem was to solve the wood joints which would create more lines and permit an openness needed for this very small space. Thus, came the idea of using 3/4" by 1-1/2" wood strips laid on the three quarter edge and bent to curvatures decided upon at the site. These strips lay upon 2"x4" deck joists. The strips were fastened by the use of spiral ringed nails which were hammered at an angle through the wood strip and into the 2"x4". The curvature at places actually cantilevered the pool edges and in other places dipped inside of it to show the original pool coping. In some of the places where it dipped inside, we created pool side planters. Some of the foliage would even touch the water's edge. A diving rock was established in this same style. At the shallow end of the pool we created an arbor over the decking and planted Bougainvillea.

Near the family area, which was outside the kitchen, a larger arbor was constructed for shade and planted with Wisteria. This arbor was lifted to a higher elevation so as not to interfere with the feeling of space. Finally the pool was drained and replastered with a green/black (originally white) which captured the reflection of all the background trees and gave the area within a marvelous, intimate feeling of a lagoon. It took the client several months of weekends to complete this project and many visits by me to advise him of methods, but the completed work was as good as any finish carpenter might expect. It has lasted well and many parties have sailed its decks."

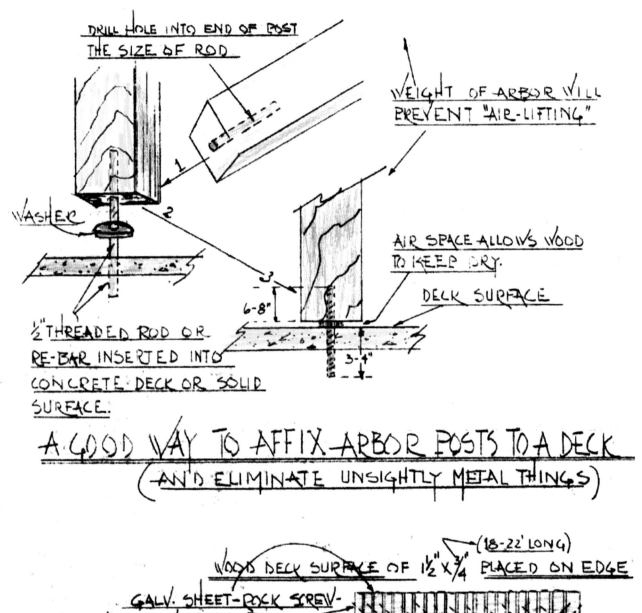

DRILL HOLE INTO END OF POST THE SIZE OF ROD

WEIGHT OF ARBOR WILL PREVENT "AIR-LIFTING"

WASHER

AIR SPACE ALLOWS WOOD TO KEEP DRY.

DECK SURFACE

6-8"

½" THREADED ROD OR RE-BAR INSERTED INTO CONCRETE DECK OR SOLID SURFACE.

3-4"

A GOOD WAY TO AFFIX ARBOR POSTS TO A DECK
(AND ELIMINATE UNSIGHTLY METAL THINGS)

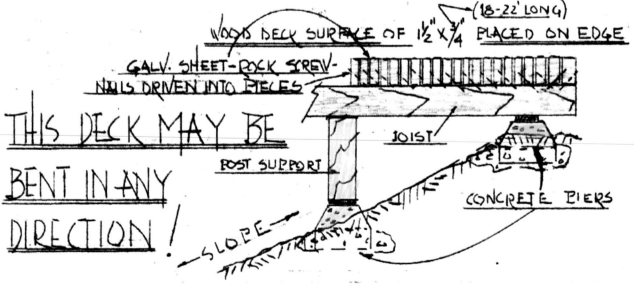

WOOD DECK SURFACE OF 1½" X ¾" PLACED ON EDGE (18-22' LONG)

GALV. SHEET-ROCK SCREW-NAILS DRIVEN INTO PIECES

THIS DECK MAY BE BENT IN ANY DIRECTION!

POST SUPPORT

JOIST

CONCRETE PIERS

SLOPE

Details here show the finishing steps to a deck and how to laminate 1"x2"'s for a bench.

Cedar blocks 4"x4"x4" have been saturated in a preservative and set on a 3½" concrete slab for stability to form this pathway.

174

Taking advantage of steep slopes, valleys, or canyons is a good way to enlarge the property by building a deck over the otherwise unused land. Let a tree or two remain for shade and character.

Every utility area must have a gate and a peep hole for the various sized dogs.

A new set of stairs was created over the old stairs! The "squeeze" style hand railing has a very comforting soft feel.

177

The stonewalls together with a mixture of quiet evergreen and dwarf shrub offer subliminal feelings of compassion while one passes by.

178

Front entrance lines and textures are practical and yet sensitive.

A patio in Carmel Valley captures the long views, quiet scenes and vines of grapes.

A clay pathway meanders and reverses through a collection of perennials with scents, flowers, and berries.
One can blindly walk through this area with ease. The boxwood hedging guides by touch and where open,
an edging board guides the foot. Touch, listen, taste, watch and feel the security.

An intermediate level connects where two separate stairs meet (See page 129).

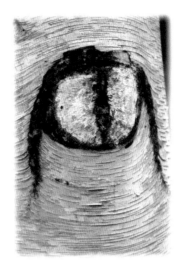

canoe Birch (Betula papyrifera)

Barking up the Birch

When reading about the Lewis and Clark expedition and marveling at this fantastic adventure into the vast primordial forests and rugged terrain of the Northwest Territory, I was reminded of my Boy Scout experiences roaming through the woods of northern Maine.

Near our camp, which was pitched close to the Canadian border and encompassed by a rather extended area of forest, I found much of what I include in my designs today. I came across small, hidden, mossy bogs filled with tiny critters hiding among twigs, huge boulders and small wild flowers. The tops of the rock formations were covered with small ferns and surrounded by the canopies of different species of trees. It seemed that, with every step taken, new vistas appeared. Each experience gave me enough to see, smell and hear to last a lifetime - and it has.

An especially awe-inspiring moment was when I came across a massive grove of canoe Birch (Betula papyrifera) that extended for a mile or so without the interruption of any other species of large trees. This was surely a phenomenon of nature. Such pockets of singular tree growth are a rare spectacle and the sight of such an extreme example was almost hallucinatory. The effect was further enhanced by a small copse of yellow Birch (Betula alleganiensis), which somehow had edged into all this heavenly whiteness. Yellow Birch, compared with the white canoe Birch, has a tighter bark, which peels off the trunk in slivers, creating a shining effect especially when moved by the wind. This action can become almost hypnotic, riveting the attention.

Birch trees, when considered for residential plantings, are more often thought of as individual entities or in small groupings. This seems to me not to be the most effective way to use them. When you place these trees individually in groups they will show off their five different bark colors: red

Yellow birch, the unheralded gem of the north woods.

Paper Birch having a quiet meeting.

(Betula nigra), yellow (Betula alleganiensis), white (Betula papyifera or jacquemonti), gray (Betula populifolia) and black Betula lenta of which this variety was used by companies which crushed its stems and branches to produce the syrup for "Birch Beer". That's right, count 'em, five. Their varied characteristics of branching, size, bark, color and even taste (Betula lenta) will add much individual and aesthetic interest to any space within a garden, be it large or small. Do not be timid about planting them close together and at different angles.

You may not always be able to tell a dog by its bark but there's no question about the birch. The Bamboos, Japanese Maples, Oaks and Poplars also are good selections, providing character and canopy when planted in rows or large clusters. The idea is to evoke a particular value through mass, color, shape and movement.

186

Under planting of ferns and low growth plants or ground covers make a wonderful setting for these Birch trees.

The use of Bamboo in mass plantings has never been popular in this country due to the plant's ability to proliferate from its spurious and shaft-like underground roots. Japanese shoguns, in their desire to repel intruders, would have the bamboo rootlets spread around the pagoda entrances which are devastatingly cruel when stepped upon. So, placing underground side barriers into the soil 18" to 24" deep will prevent their spread and easily contain the roots.

Accordingly, the Bamboos should be used without hesitation, as they are very expressive in both sight and sound. When traveling in Japan and staying in local countryside homes or inns, the quiet rustling sounds of the Bamboo forests are entrancing. But you don't have to travel that far, you can have the same experience right in your own backyard. 🌱

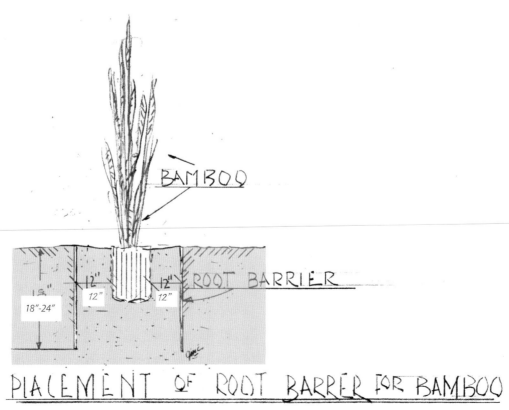

BAMBOO

ROOT BARRIER

12"
12"
12"
12"

18"
18"-24"

PLACEMENT OF ROOT BARRER FOR BAMBOO

188

ROSE GARDEN

BAMBOO

MINIATURE

GARAGE ROOF OVERHANG

THIS AREA TO BE MOUNDED DOWN TO LAKE EDGE STONE PLANTING

PATH

LOW STONE WALL W/ 6' WROUGHT IRON FENCE

SCULPTURE

TERMINAL FINIAL

CONC. STEPS DOWN

ENTRANCE WALK
(SEE DETAIL FOR FRESCO PAVEMENT)

FR ENTRANCE ROOF OVERHANG

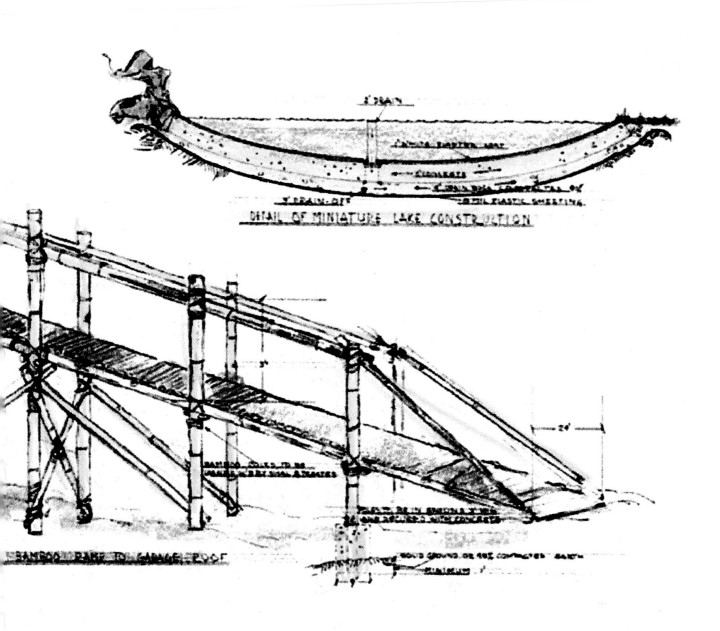

DETAIL OF MINIATURE LAKE CONSTRUCTION

BAMBOO RAMP TO GARAGE ROOF

SECTION

TYPICAL ENTRANCE PAVEMENT & STEP DETAIL

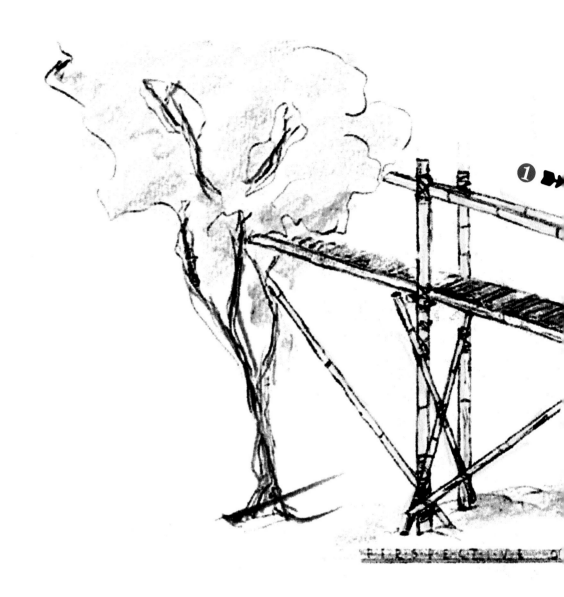

PERSPECTIVE O

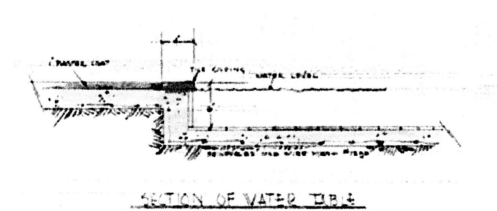

SECTION OF WATER TABLE

NOTE:

TYPICAL WALL

A large entrance area consisting of front walk with a inlaid intaglio Poppy design, leading to a front entrance Watertable of oversize flat walking stones on the water surface. A miniature Lake and setting with a significant stone Monolith for reflection. Garage roof parking and employing a alternate garden entrance of a Bamboo Ramp (1) to the Moss and Garden Terrace.

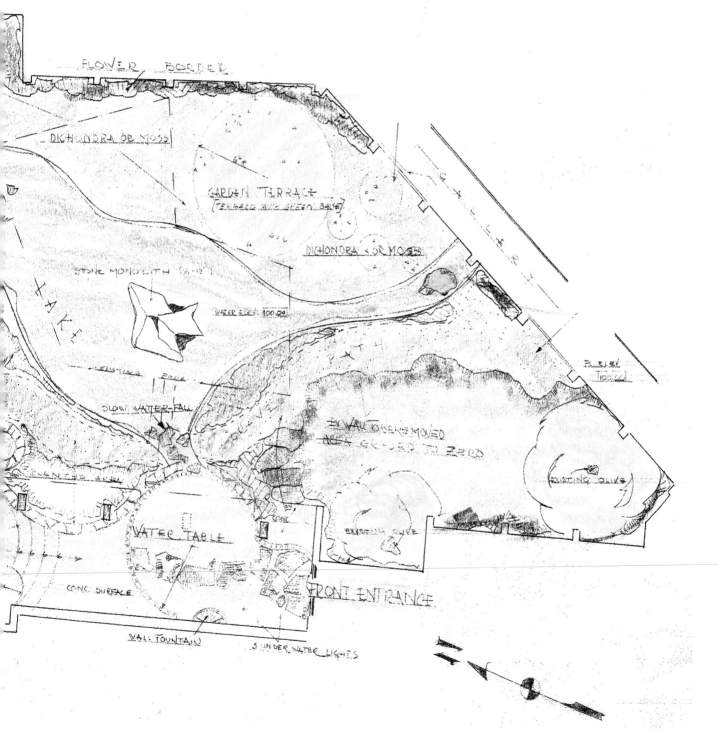

PLEASE LIFT →

Fagus sylvestris ...the very stalwart European Beech with all its knots and curly-cues ...and messages from the past lovers! >>

<< *Pinus strobus v. fastigiata. A pyramidal White pine. Good for hard to figure corners.*

193

Barefeet love this path to the secluded spa.

Evoking Emotional Responses into Your Landscape Design

From time immemorial our environment has given to all humans on Earth the pleasures of visual and meaningful fullness of life. Nature surely has evoked responses in us, and we individually have felt the spiritual and personal need to react in kind within characteristics given to our minds and souls.

It is so within the practice of the landscape designer to look for personal characteristics and traits from the client which can be interchanged amongst the real landscape to emulate human feelings. Thus having some knowledge of what the human character before you has offered in personality insight, one can profile traits with this knowledge into the natural elements of design which evoke subliminal messages into a natural art form.

The late neo-Kantian Dutch philosopher, Herman Dooyeweerd, devised a system for classifying all aspects of reality, which he early on called "sovereign spheres" and later referred to as "law spheres" or "modalities," that helps us see the interrelatedness of one basic element in creation with each other. Dooyeweerd charted fifteen such least-common denominators, building from the lowest and most universal number to what he considered the highest, the most peculiarly human. A brief perusal of Dooyeweerd's map of creation will not only help us see where landscape architecture may fit into the larger scheme of things, but will be useful later on for planning architectural repertories (design programs) as well.

First, let's look again at the 15 modalities (aspects of all creation) in terms of what I call possible natural repertories. A repertory, as I'm using it, is a combination of landscape features; a collection a display made up of components close in meaning to a "scenario." These are not meant to be thought of as the only possibilities, but rather as one of several chosen from a myriad of possibilities.

The **numerical** modality can be represented by repetitively structured repertories: a long row of narrow upright trees or an even line of statuary, architectural dentil ornamentation or columns, ordered parallel rows in a vegetable garden, and a trail or path comprised of single stepping stones are possibilities. See pages: 16, 18, 44, 48, 87, 110, 124 upper, and 144.

The **spatial** modality suggests and is suggested by representations of timelessness: a long open view with no boundaries; elevation-a high viewpoint offering no individual material interruptions. See pages: 6, 7, 19, 59, 130, 138, 164, 168, and 179.

The **kinematic** modality, energy, can be suggested by converging or diverging lines, as a stream with an island in it; long or short curving lines; any appearance of authority.

The **physical** modality is the irreducible element of mass, and can be suggested by a rocky area with a solitary water fountain (also representing physical force), or a solitary object like a specimen oak. Another approach to representing the physical dimension of reality would be devoting a section of a landscape to exercising or sports activity. See pages: 1 upper, 36, 171, and 193.

The **biological** modality can be represented by physiological or botanical arrangements: an old stump, a forest floor, lichen growth, tide pools, plant breeding or growing. See pages: 3, 45, 116, 150, 161, 175, 177, 184, and 186.

The **psychical**, the part of creation having to do with thought, can be represented or suggested by a sunken moss garden or pool enclosed by soft foliage; anything indicating a quiet attitude or sensitivity. See pages: 23, 43, 45, 52, 59, 74, 84, 117, 126, 138, 150, 164, 180, and 186.

The **analytical logical** modality can be suggested by formality or balanced informality, as a fulcrum design. Any design that makes the observer think or suggests subtle or hidden nuances would be an appropriate representation or response to this element. See pages: 92, 110, 144, and 155.

The **historical** modality is suggested by designs with a sense of antiquity and ones that imply sophistication and knowledge. The use of such fine art as sculpture and classic architectural details adds refinement and sensitivity to a space reflecting a sense of history. See pages: 105, 108, 109, 117, 143, 147, and 154.

The **linguistic** modality is suggested by landscape elements appealing to the senses of sight, smell, taste, or sound. They elicit comment and description. Likewise, as in an arboretum, name tags identifying the flora are specific uses of the linguistic sphere. Use of colors or sound to stimulate memories might also be appropriate. See pages: 12, 31, 35, 47, 49, 50, 56, and 57.

The **social** aspect of reality can be represented in the garden by having the whole family participate in planning and upkeep, and by sharing plots in community gardens for raising vegetables. Front yards, used by the family with porch swings and other furniture, were common in close communities but seem largely a thing of the past in loose societies. They were social in that they were a meeting place between the home and the world, a place to watch the world go by and occasionally greet it or welcome it. See pages: 5, 24 upper, 43, 44, 47, 60, 89, 118, 125, and 180.

The economic aspect of the landscape can be represented by low cost maintenance, or thrift in its design and implementation. Use of trees bearing fruit as well as providing shade and ornamentation and growing vegetables, either in whole gardens or in small isolated plantings, are direct applications of the garden to the personal economy. See pages: 1, 3, 29, 60, 62, 93, 108, 116, 158, 163, 177, and 179.

The aesthetic aspect is served by any use of planning, arranging, pruning, weeding, organization and discussion of human survival and its optimization. See pages: 61, 118, 132, 137, 150, 152, 175, and 179. 🌼

Sample Plans & Detail Sketches

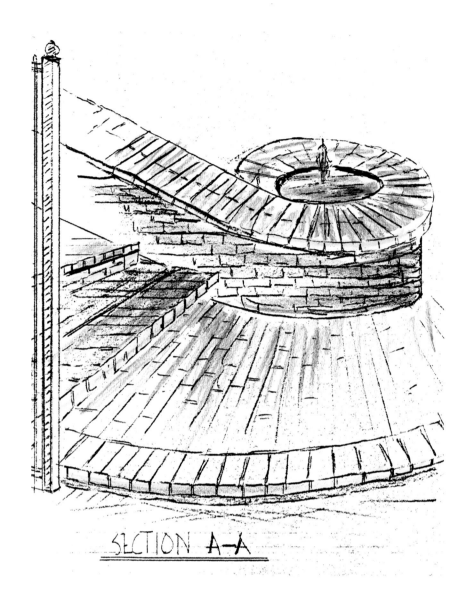

SECTION A-A

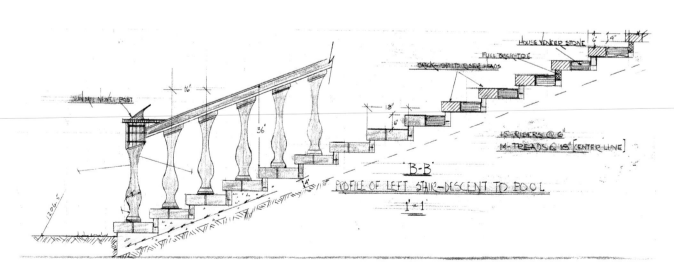

SUNDAIL NEWEL POST

16"

36"

1206.5

HOUSE VENEER STONE

FULL BRICK TOE

BRICK-SPLIT RISER HEADS

18"

6"

15 RISERS @ 6"
14 TREADS @ 18" [CENTER LINE]

B-B
PROFILE OF LEFT STAIR-DESCENT TO POOL
1'=1'

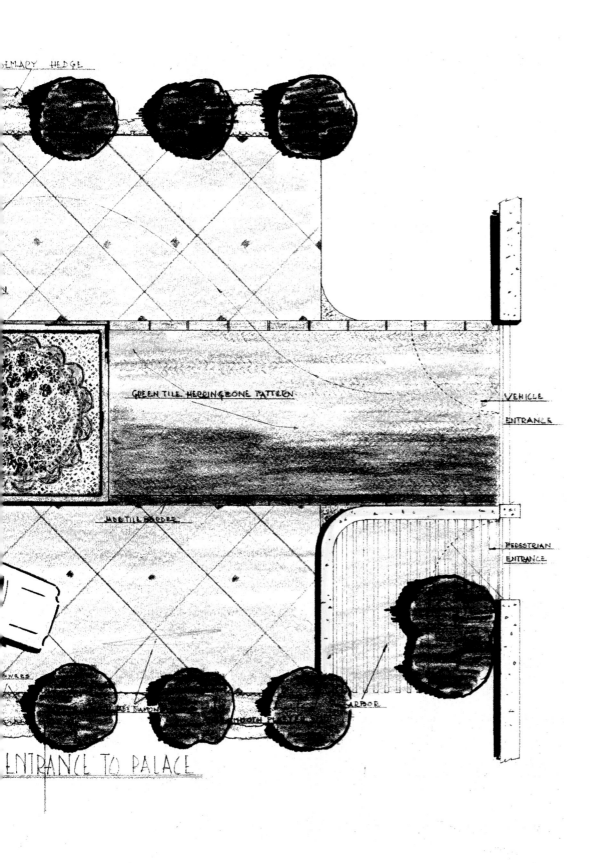

ROSEMARY HEDGE

GREEN TILE HERRINGBONE PATTERN

VEHICLE ENTRANCE

MOB TILE BORDER

PEDESTRIAN ENTRANCE

ARBOR

ENTRANCE TO PALACE

PALACE COURT-YARD DESIGN

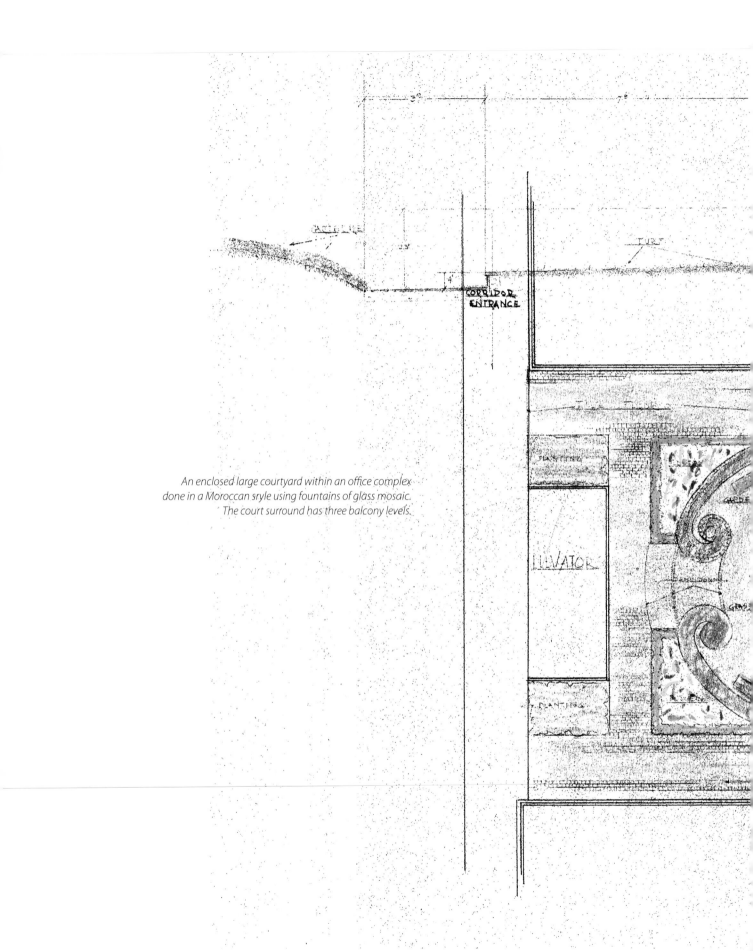

*An enclosed large courtyard within an office complex
done in a Moroccan sryle using fountains of glass mosaic.
The court surround has three balcony levels.*

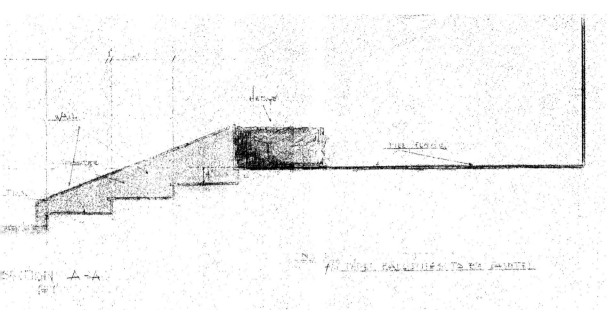

SECTION A-A

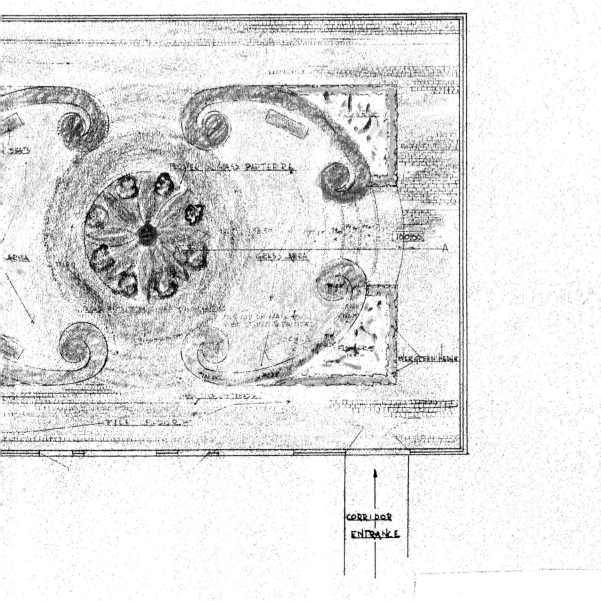

FLOWER ON GRASS PARTERRE

GRASS AREA

A

EVERGREEN HEDGE

CORRIDOR
ENTRANCE

PLEASE LIFT →

FLOWERS

FLOWERS

MOSIAC FOUNTA

FOUNTAIN

FLOWERS

DETAIL OF DOOR FOR PEDESTRIAN ENTRANCE

COURT-YARD

DETAIL OF FOUNTAIN MOSAIC PATTERNS

SUGGESTED P

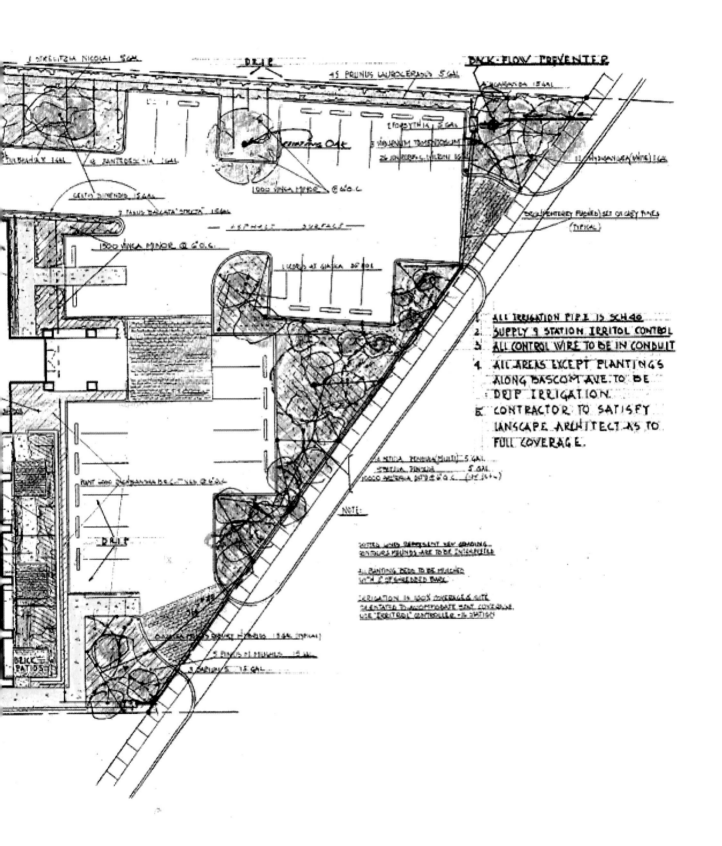

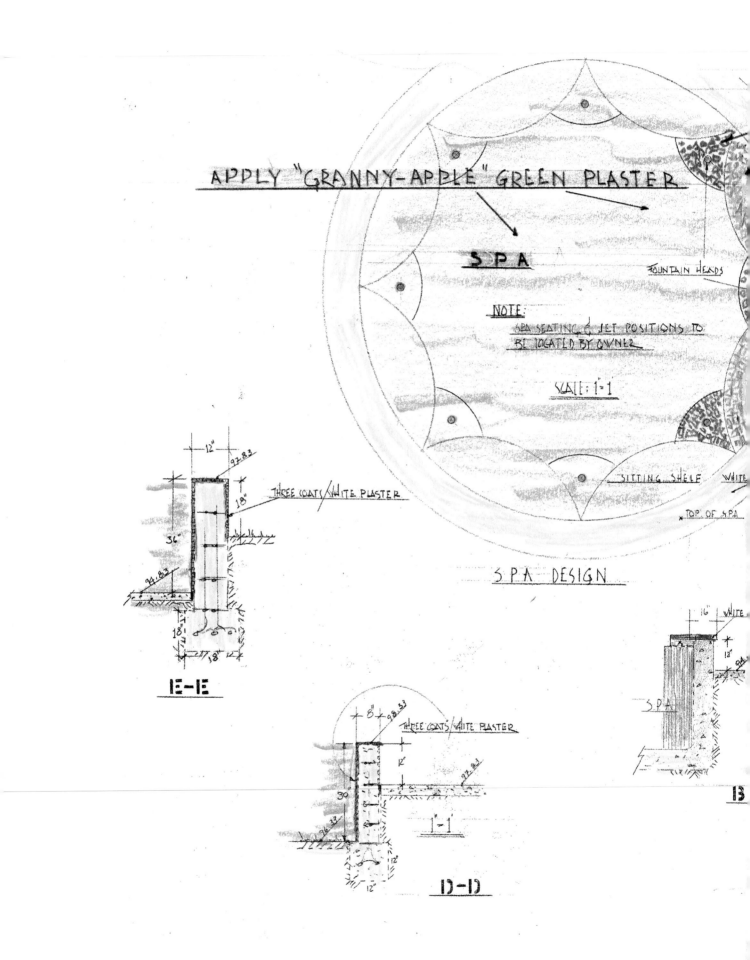

APPLY "GRANNY-APPLE" GREEN PLASTER

S P A

FOUNTAIN HEADS

NOTE:
SPA SEATING & JET POSITIONS TO
BE LOCATED BY OWNER

SCALE: 1"=1'

SITTING SHELF   WHITE

TOP OF SPA

S P A   DESIGN

THREE COATS/WHITE PLASTER

E-E

THREE COATS/WHITE PLASTER

1"-1'

D-D

SPA

B

205

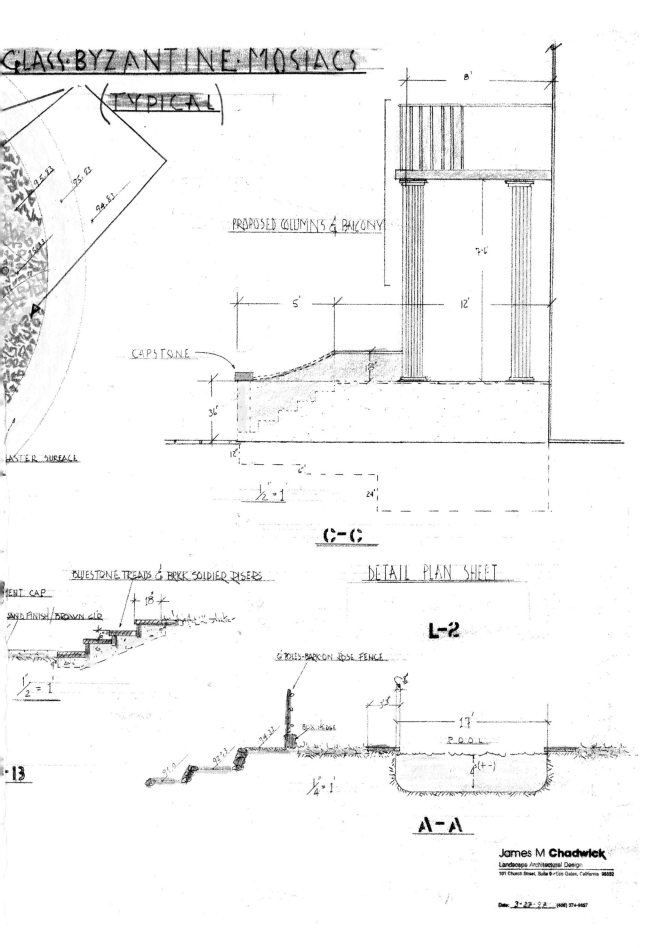

GLASS·BYZANTINE·MOSIACS

(TYPICAL)

95.83
95.83
94.83

A

PROPOSED COLUMNS & BALCONY

8'

7-6"

12'

5'

CAPSTONE

18"

36"

12"

6'

24'

PLASTER SURFACE

½" = 1'

C-C

BLUESTONE TREADS & BRICK SOLDIER RISERS

DETAIL PLAN SHEET

CEMENT CAP

18"

SAND FINISH / BROWN CLR

L-2

½" = 1'

6 ROLES-BARK ON ROSE FENCE

BOX HEDGE

13"

17'

P·O·O·L

94.33

92.33

13

91.0

¼" = 1'

4'(+-)

A-A

James M **Chadwick**
Landscape Architectural Design
101 Church Street, Suite 9 · Los Gatos, California 95032

Date: 3·27·92   (408) 374-8857

PLEASE LIFT →

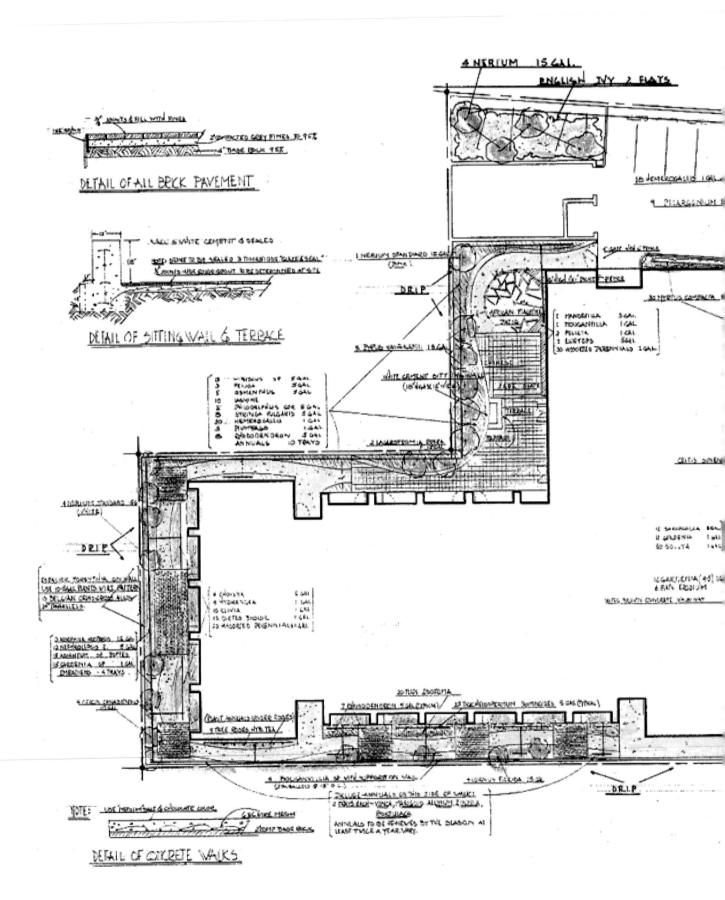

DETAIL OF ALL BRICK PAVEMENT

DETAIL OF SITTING WALL & TERRACE

DETAIL OF CONCRETE WALKS

207

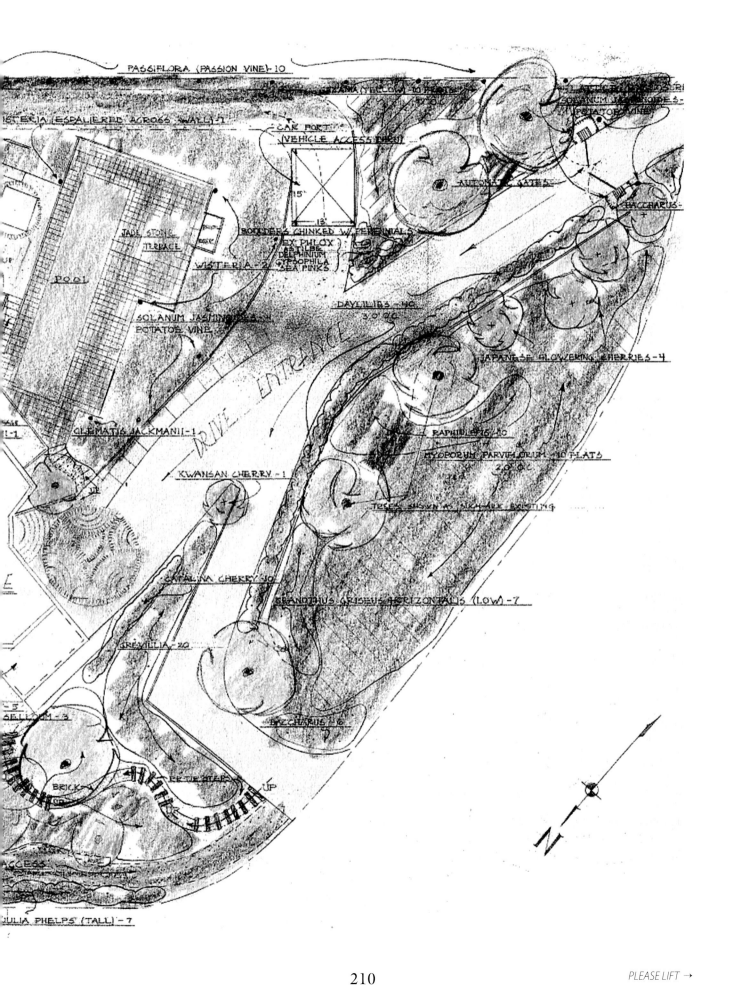

PASSIFLORA (PASSION VINE)-10

WISTERIA (ESPALIERED ACROSS WALLS)-7

CAR PORT
(VEHICLE ACCESS SIGN)

15'

13'

JADE STONE
TERRACE

POOL

WISTERIA-2

SOLANUM JASMINOIDEA
(POTATOE VINE)

CLEMATIS JACKMANII-1

KWANSAN CHERRY-1

CATALINA CHERRY-10

GREVILLIA-20

BRICK-X

JULIA PHELPS (TALL)-7

BOULDERS CHINKED W/ PERENNIALS
EX PHLOX
ASTILBE
DELPHINIUM
GYPSOPHILA
SEA PINKS

DAYLILIES-40
3.0' O.C.

JAPANESE FLOWERING CHERRIES-4

RAPHIOLEPIS-40

MYOPORUM PARVIFLORUM -40 FLATS
2.0' O.C.

TREES SHOWN AS DARK ARE EXISTING

CEANOTHUS GRISEUS HORIZONTALIS (LOW)-7

BACCHARUS-6

BACCHARUS

AUTOMATIC GATES

SOLANUM JASMINOIDES-
(POTATOE VINE)

N

PLEASE LIFT →

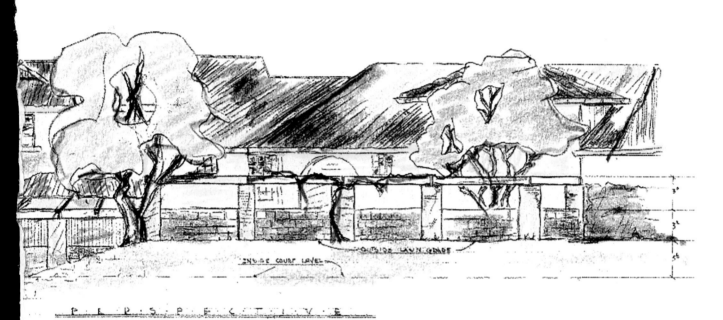

INSIDE COURT LEVEL

OUTSIDE LAWN GRADE

P·E·R·S·P·E·C·T·I·V·E

SCALE ½"=1'

212

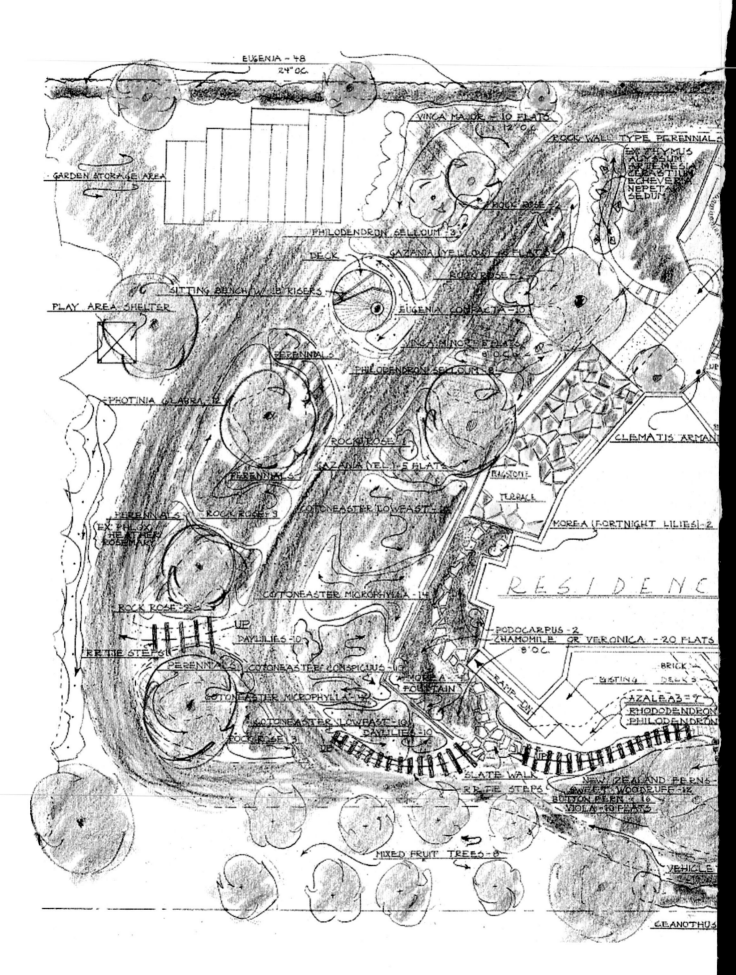

EUGENIA - 48
24" O.C.

VINCA MAJOR - 10 FLATS
12" O.C.

ROCK WALL TYPE PERENNIAL
EX THYMUS
ALYSSUM
ARTEMESIA
CERASTIUM
ECHEVERIA
NEPETA
SEDUM

GARDEN STORAGE AREA

ROCK ROSE

PHILODENDRON SELLOUM - 3

DECK

GAZANIA (YELLOW) - 5 FLATS

ROCK ROSE

SITTING BENCH W/ 18" RISERS

PLAY AREA SHELTER

EUGENIA COMPACTA - 10

VINCA MINOR 6 FLATS
8" O.C.

PERENNIALS

PHILODENDRON SELLOUM - 8

PHOTINIA GLABRA - 12

CLEMATIS ARMAN

ROCK ROSE

FLAGSTONE

GAZANIA (YEL.) - 5 FLATS

PERENNIALS

TERRACE

MOREA (FORTNIGHT LILIES) - 2

PERENNIALS
EX PHLOX
HEATHER
ROSEMARY

ROCK ROSE - 3

COTONEASTER 'LOWFAST' -

COTONEASTER MICROPHYLLA - 14

RESIDENC

PODOCARPUS - 2

ROCK ROSE - 2

CHAMOMILE OR VERONICA - 20 FLATS
8" O.C.

UP

DAYLILIES - 10

BRICK

R.R. TIE STEPS

PERENNIALS

COTONEASTER CONSPICUUS -

MOREA - 4
FOUNTAIN

RAMP DN

EXISTING DECKS

COTONEASTER MICROPHYLLA -

AZALEAS - 9

COTONEASTER 'LOWFAST' - 10

RHODODENDRON

ROCK ROSE - 3

DAYLILIES - 10

PHILODENDRON

UP

SLATE WALK

NEW ZEALAND FERNS

R.R. TIE STEPS

SWEET WOODRUFF - 12

BUTTON FERN - 16

VIOLA - 10 FLATS

MIXED FRUIT TREES - 8

VEHICLE

CEANOTHUS

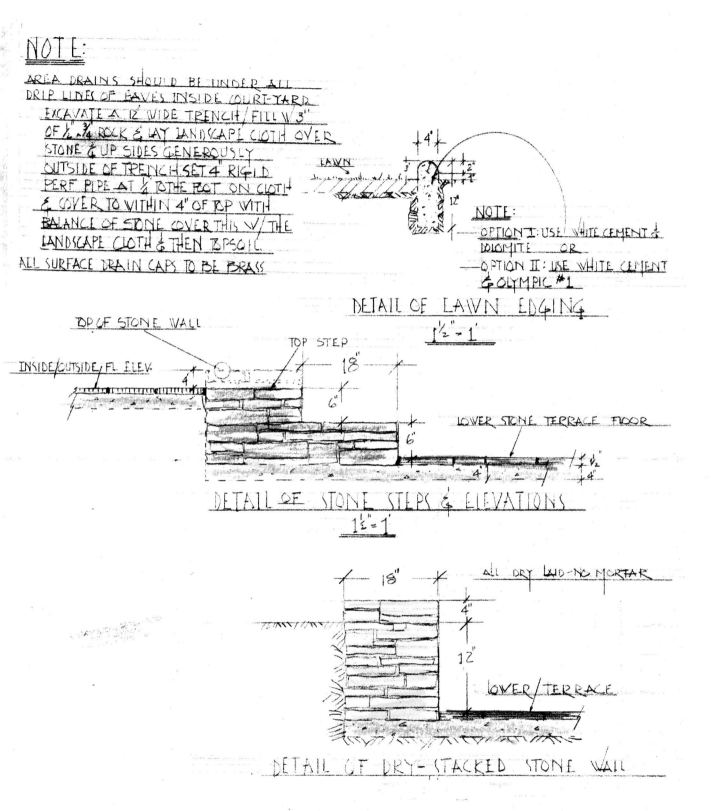

NOTE:

AREA DRAINS SHOULD BE UNDER ALL
DRIP LINES OF EAVES INSIDE COURT-YARD
EXCAVATE A 12" WIDE TRENCH / FILL W/ 3"
OF ½ - ¾ ROCK & LAY LANDSCAPE CLOTH OVER
STONE & UP SIDES GENEROUSLY
OUTSIDE OF TRENCH SET 4" RIGID
PERF PIPE AT ½ TO THE FOOT ON CLOTH
& COVER TO WITHIN 4" OF TOP WITH
BALANCE OF STONE OVER THIS W/ THE
LANDSCAPE CLOTH & THEN TOPSOIL.
ALL SURFACE DRAIN CAPS TO BE BRASS

LAWN

4"

2"

12"

NOTE:

OPTION I: USE WHITE CEMENT &
DOLOMITE   OR
OPTION II: USE WHITE CEMENT
& OLYMPIC #1

DETAIL OF LAWN EDGING

1½" = 1'

TOP OF STONE WALL

INSIDE/OUTSIDE FL. ELEV.

TOP STEP

18"

6"

6"

4"

LOWER STONE TERRACE FLOOR

½"

4"

DETAIL OF STONE STEPS & ELEVATIONS

1½" = 1'

18"

ALL DRY LAID-NO MORTAR

4"

12"

LOWER/TERRACE

DETAIL OF DRY-STACKED STONE WALL

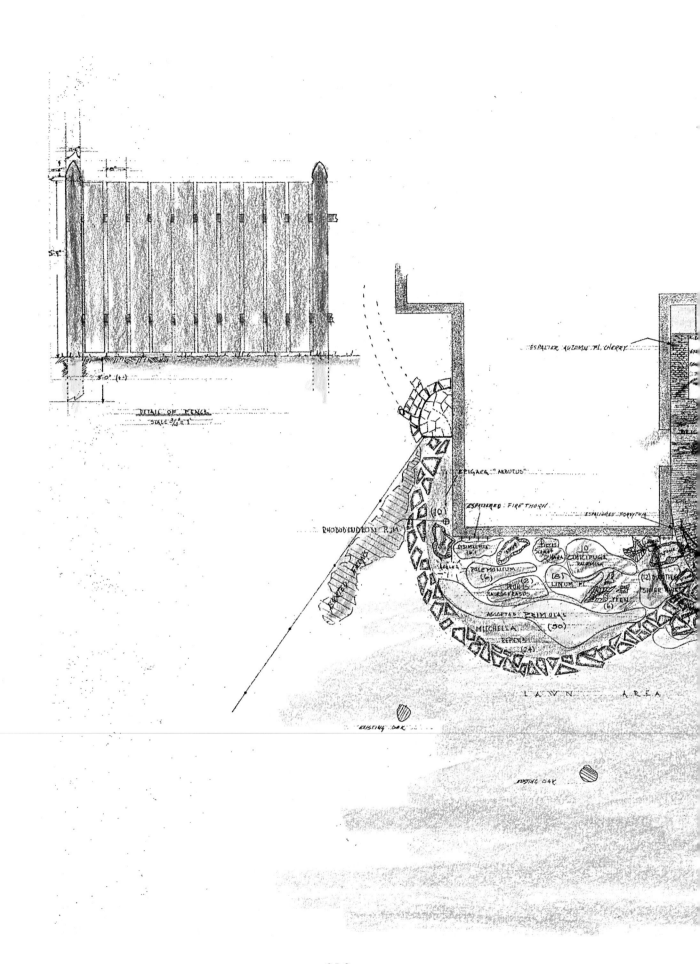

DETAIL OF FENCE
SCALE 3/4" = 1'

3'-0" (±)

ESPALIER AUTUMN FL. CHERRY

EPIGAEA "ARBUTUS"

ESPALIERED FIRETHORN

ESPALIERED FORSYTHIA

RHODODENDRON R.M.

POLEMONIUM
(6)

PRUNUS
LAUROCERASUS
(2)

LINUM FL.
(8)

CIMICIFUGE
RACEMOSA

(10)

FERN
(6)

ASSORTED PRIMULAS
(50)

MITCHELLA
REPENS
(24)

LAWN   AREA

EXISTING OAK

EXISTING OAK

213

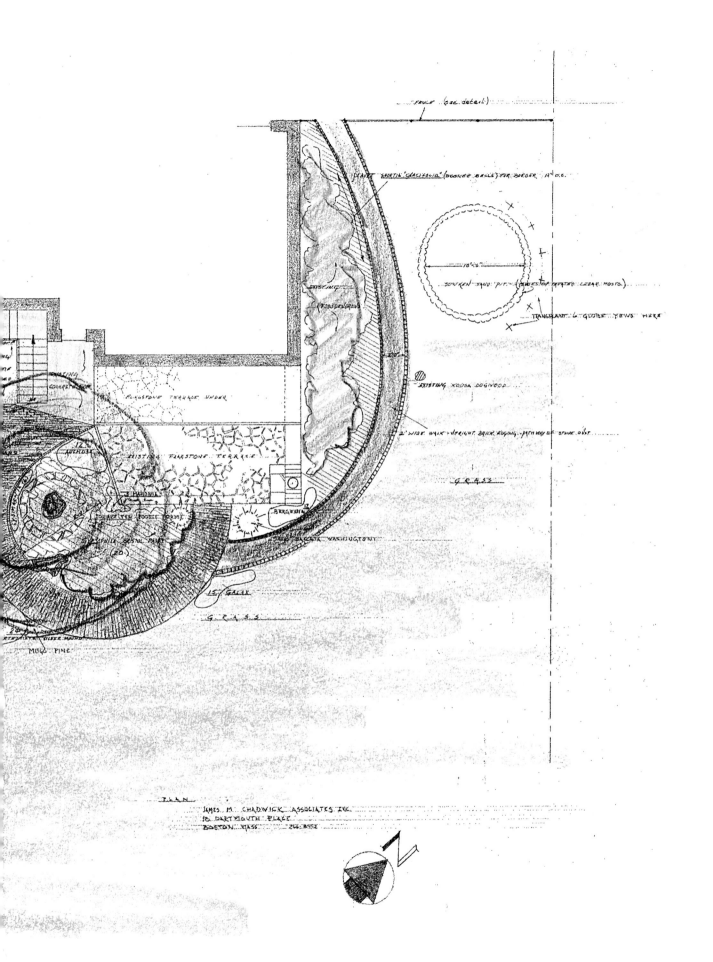

TRILLS (see detail)

PLANT "SHORTIA" "GRACILFOLIA" (OCONEE BELLS) PER BORDER 18" O.C.

EXISTING
(RHODODENDRON)

SUNKEN SAND PIT (SIDES OF TREATED CEDAR POSTS)

TRANSPLANT 6 GLOBE YEWS HERE

EXISTING KOUSA DOGWOOD

2' WIDE WALK UPRIGHT BRICK EDGING PATHWAY OF STONE DUST

GRASS

FLAGSTONE TERRACE UNDER

EXISTING FLAGSTONE TERRACE

3 MAHONIA

TOPIARY YEW (GLOBE FORM)

BERBERIS

ALBIZIA WASHINGTONII

15 GALAX

GRASS

MUGO PINE

PLAN

JAMES M. CHADWICK ASSOCIATES INC
10 DARTMOUTH PLACE
BOSTON MASS   266.8952

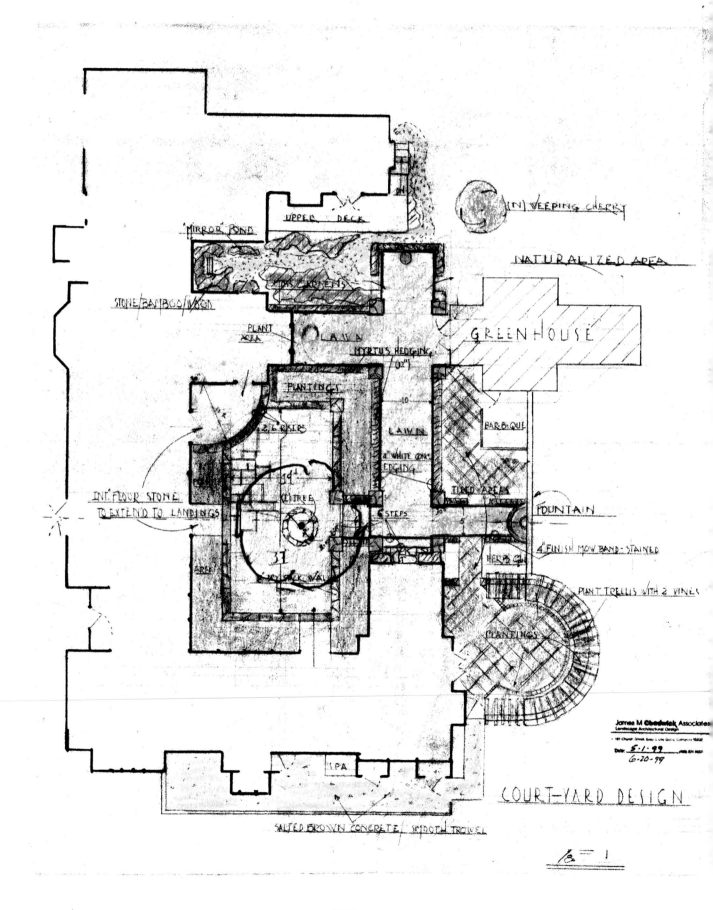

COURT-YARD DESIGN

215